George Washington

FOR KIDS

George Washington

FOR KIDS

His Life and Times
21 ACTIVITIES

BRANDON MARIE MILLER

CHICAGO REVIEW PRESS

To my parents, who long ago first took me to Mount
Vernon, Yorktown, Valley Forge, Williamsburg . . .

Library of Congress Cataloging-in-Publication Data
Miller, Brandon Marie.
  George Washington for kids : his life and times with 21 activities / Brandon Marie
Miller.—1st ed.
      p. cm.
  Includes bibliographical references and index.
  ISBN-13: 978-1-55652-655-8
  ISBN-10: 1-55652-655-5
  1. Washington, George, 1732-1799–Juvenile literature. 2.
Presidents–United States–Biography–Juvenile literature. 3.
Generals–United States–Biography–Juvenile literature. 4. Creative activities and seat
work. I. Title.

  E312.66.M545 2007
  973.4'1092–dc22
  [B]

                                                                        2006031674

Cover design: Joan Sommers

Cover images:
  "Portrait of George Washington on American one dollar note"
  © Photolibrary/Alamy

  "Young George Washington working as a surveyor in Virginia Colony"
  © North Wind Picture Archives/Alamy

  "George Washington at Princeton"
  © Visual Arts Library (London)/Alamy

  "Mount Vernon in Virginia" engraving by Francis Jukes
  Library of Congress

  Feather quill pen with ink
  © Brand X Pictures/Alamy

Interior design: Scott Rattray

Published by Chicago Review Press, Incorporated
814 North Franklin Street
Chicago, Illinois 60610
ISBN 978-1-55652-655-8
Printed in the United States of America
5 4 3 2

Contents

Acknowledgments

aterial from *The Papers of George Washington* are reprinted with permission of the University of Virginia Press.

My thanks to the staff and historic interpreters at George Washington's Mount Vernon Estate and Gardens. Thanks to Paul Miller for his encouragement and computer expertise and to the Chael family and Peg Schlenker for their help in testing activities. And to Neal and Justine Hendy for listening to many George Washington stories over the past few years.

Time Line

1732	George Washington is born February 22, in Virginia
1743	Washington's father, Augustine, dies
1748	Washington makes his first trip west, as part of a surveying mission
1752	Washington's brother Lawrence dies
1753	21-year-old Washington sent to warn the French out of the Ohio country
1754	Washington fights a skirmish with the French that begins the French and Indian War; surrenders Fort Necessity to the French
1755	Washington serves under British general Edward Braddock during the Battle of Monongahela; appointed head of Virginia forces assigned to protect the frontier
1758	Washington serves in the Forbes campaign against Fort Duquesne; elected to Virginia's House of Burgesses
1759	Washington marries Martha Dandridge Custis and settles at Mount Vernon
1765	Britain pays down war debt by taxing the colonies; the Stamp Act is passed spurring riots in the colonies
1767	Townshend Acts ignite protests and boycotts of British goods
1773	Washington's stepdaughter, Patsy Custis, dies; Boston citizens dump taxed tea into Boston Harbor
1774	Washington promotes a boycott of British goods; serves as a Virginia delegate to the First Continental Congress

1775	American Revolution begins when colonists fight British troops in Massachusetts; Washington named commander in chief of the Continental Army
1776	Washington is defeated and retreats from New York; army crosses the Delaware River and surprises Hessian troops at Trenton
1777	American victory at Battle of Princeton; Washington defeated at Brandywine and Germantown; winter camp at Valley Forge, Pennsylvania
1778	Alliance made with France; Battle of Monmouth
1779–80	Army suffers through winter at Morristown, New Jersey
1781	Washington, with French aid, defeats Cornwallis at Yorktown, Virginia; Washington's stepson, Jacky, dies
1783	Treaty of Paris ending the war signed; Washington resigns his commission before Congress and returns to Mount Vernon
1787	Washington serves as president of the Constitutional Convention, where a new plan of government is written
1789	Washington sworn in as the first president of the United States; the French Revolution begins
1791	Washington chooses a site on the Potomac River for the new federal city
1792	Washington elected to a second term; political split widens between cabinet members Hamilton and Jefferson
1793	France and England are at war; Washington issues Proclamation of Neutrality
1794	Whiskey Rebellion erupts in western Pennsylvania; Jay Treaty is signed in England
1795	Treaty with Spain allows the United States to use the Mississippi River
1796	Washington's Farewell Address is published
1797	Washington steps down from the presidency
1799	George Washington dies at Mount Vernon

Note to Readers

Many of George Washington's diaries, letters, and other papers have survived for over 200 years. So throughout this book, many of the words you'll read were written by Washington himself, written in joy, in anger, in despair, and in pride. A real man, not a cold marble statue, wrote these words. Can you see Washington, in flickering candle flame, dipping his quill pen in ink and writing the very words you read? Do you feel a connection to a real person? Think about it.

Research materials that actually come from a certain historic period, such as diaries, letters, paintings, clothes, tools, and newspapers, are called "primary sources." They were written or used by people of that time. Spelling, grammar, and punctuation have all changed over the centuries. A letter looking much like an *f* meant an *s* in George Washington's time. To see some of Washington's papers for yourself, go online to the Library of Congress (www.loc.gov) or the University of Virginia (www.virginia.edu).

Preface

A Young Virginian Sets the World on Fire

May 28, 1754

The rain pounded down, the night black as pitch. Through darkness the Virginia militia soldiers struggled to find a path. They crashed through trees, lost their way, stumbled into one another in the Pennsylvania wilderness. At daybreak they reached the camp of Native American leader Half King and his warriors. Half King and the militia leader, a newly appointed lieutenant colonel at age 22, agreed to strike an encampment of French soldiers in a ravine a few miles away.

The Virginians and Indians surrounded the camp, screened by huge boulders and trees. Smoke from breakfast fires drifted upward. Suddenly, a French soldier spied the red coats of the militia looming above and cried out, sending men racing for their guns. The young Virginian ordered his men to fire. The sudden blast of muskets thundered down the ravine. The skirmish, the young Virginian's first battle, lasted only 15 minutes.

He climbed down ready to accept the French surrender. Ten French soldiers lay dead, including French commander Joseph Coulon de Villiers, Sieur de Jumonville. But instead of surrender, chaos erupted. Native American warriors swarmed down the ravine to claim their trophies of war, the scalps of the dead. French prisoners yelled at the young Virginian and shoved papers in his face.

He listened as his two interpreters rapidly turned French and Native American into English. His French interpreter stood between the Virginian and the angry French, translating as fast as he could. The French claimed they had come on a peaceful diplomatic mission–they were not a war party, not spies! They waved their diplomatic papers as proof. They'd been sent to warn the British off the Ohio Valley lands claimed by the king of France. The young Virginian, accused the French, had murdered an ambassador!

On that May morning an unsteady peace existed between old enemies France and Great Britain. The young Virginian's actions in the Pennsylvania wilderness exploded into an international affair. His orders sparked a war that spread across North America and Europe. The son of Britain's prime minister noted, "The volley fired by a young Virginian in the backwoods of America set the world on fire."

That summer of 1754 few people would have bet the young Virginian's future held any glimmer of fame, honor, or greatness. His name was George Washington.

George Washington as a young man.

George Washington

FOR KIDS

1

"Began My Journey"

February winds blew across Virginia's Potomac River and ruffled the waters of Popes Creek. Augustine Washington's home, nestled among tall trees, overlooked the creek. "Gus" had built the small house near lands first owned by his grandfather John Washington 75 years before.

Four generations of Washingtons lay buried nearby. Gus's first wife, Jane, rested there, too, beneath a gravestone already scoured by the wind. Jane's death had left Gus with two sons and a daughter to raise. He needed a new wife to help manage Lawrence, Austin, Jane, and Popes Creek farm.

When Is Washington's Birthday?

In 1752 Great Britain corrected their calendar to catch up with the rest of the world. The change pushed everything ahead by 11 days. So George Washington's birthday changed from February 11 to February 22. During his lifetime George often celebrated his birthday on both days!

In 1800, Mason Locke Weems wrote a biography of George Washington. He created one of the most famous legends in American folklore. Six-year-old George has taken his new hatchet and splintered his father's cherry tree. When Gus Washington confronts his son about the damage, George replies: "I can't tell a lie, Pa: you know I can't tell a lie. I did cut it with my hatchet."

Courtesy of the Mount Vernon Ladies' Association

A year after Jane's death Gus married Mary Ball. Around ten o'clock in the morning on February 11, 1732, Mary gave birth to another Washington son they named George.

Mary and Gus's family grew year by year. George, their oldest child, welcomed a sister named Betty and three brothers, Samuel, John Augustine, and Charles. George's half sister, Jane, died. When George was three Gus moved the family up the Potomac River to another farm, Little Hunting Creek Plantation. George's two half brothers, Lawrence and Austin, had left Virginia for school in England.

Home at Ferry Farm

Like most Virginians, Gus Washington earned his living as a farmer, or "planter." But he also worked as a partner in an iron works. In 1738

This 19th-century illustration shows young George with his mother, Mary.

Courtesy of the Mount Vernon Ladies' Association

Play a Game of Quoits

Quoits was a popular ring toss game played by children and adults, similar to today's game of horseshoes. The pin and rings were most commonly made of iron and could be very heavy. Loops of rope were sometimes used in place of iron rings.

Materials

Old newspaper
2 1-gallon plastic milk jugs
Sand
2 14-inch dowel rods
4 pieces 21-inch-long rope
Duct tape

Using rolled newspaper as a funnel, fill the milk jugs halfway with sand. Stick the dowel rods into the sand to make your pins.

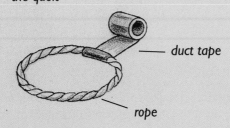

the quoit

duct tape

rope

Make a circle out of each piece of rope. Tape the circle together with duct tape. You can wrap duct tape around the entire circle if you wish. This makes your quoit.

Place the milk jugs at least 10 feet apart. A player stands next to each pin. Each player has two quoits. Take turns tossing your quoits. A quoit ringing the dowel rod earns 5 points; a quoit leaning against the jug earns 3 points. If no one rings or leans, the quoit closest to the jug earns 1 point. The first person to get 21 points wins.

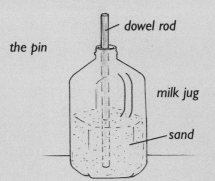

the pin

dowel rod

milk jug

sand

the family packed their wagons and moved again, this time closer to the Accokeek Iron Furnace. From his new home, called the Home Farm and later Ferry Farm, six-year-old George scampered down to the Rappahannock River, a playground for fishing, swimming, and skipping stones across the water. Beyond the river lay Fredericksburg, a growing village with a tobacco warehouse, a stone prison, a half-built church, a courthouse, and a few homes. Ships from England anchored along the wooden wharf that jutted into the river.

Two blows hit the Washington family in 1740. George's baby sister, Mildred, died and the family's home burned to the ground. Like most houses at this time, Ferry Farm's kitchen stood separate from the main house as a fire precaution. But with large open fireplaces providing a home's only heat and candle flames the only light, fire loomed as a constant hazard. With their home destroyed, George and his family crowded into the one-room kitchen while the house was rebuilt.

The Washingtons' new house had four rooms downstairs and two more above. They lived a comfortable life, but Gus was not considered a man of wealth, influence, or power. George Washington lived in a society where every person knew his or her place. The British king ruled at the top of society dressed in rich velvets and silks. A slave stood at the very bottom clad in rough-woven cloth. People believed a "gentleman of good fortune" or a "man of quality" or a "lady of the highest rank" were better than common folk. Colonists lived in a world where masters ruled over servants, men ruled over women, and parents ruled over children.

George must have gazed into one of the family's prized possessions—a mirror, or "looking glass." The looking glass in Ferry Farm's hall, the home's finest room, reflected a tall boy with reddish-brown hair, steely blue eyes, and a long, straight nose.

Only wealthy Virginians could afford real privacy. In most homes a family shared bedrooms and beds, and even a servant or two might snooze with the family. The Washingtons owned 11 bedsteads they could set up in any room, especially when visitors arrived. Three beds stood in the parlor. One four-poster bed sported long curtains that could be closed for warmth and a little privacy. To dress their beds, the family owned 6 pairs of good sheets, 10 "lesser" pairs of sheets, and 16 pillowcases.

Tobacco and Slave Culture

Virginians raised tobacco, the colony's main crop. People even used the dried leaves in place of money; Gus paid 5,500 pounds of tobacco to build Ferry Farm. Tobacco required hours of labor to baby the tender seedlings, weed the fields, pick greedy worms off the plants, then harvest and dry the tobacco leaves.

Once a year, workers packed the dried leaves into large barrels, called hogsheads. The hogsheads were then rolled or carted to waiting ships and transported to English markets. Planters hired London agents to sell their tobacco, order goods for them, and ship the merchandise and any leftover money back to Virginia. Barrels and crates of clothing, toys, dishes, books, food, farm tools, and even carriages, arrived in the colony the following year. But agents often cheated the colonists by charging for top-quality goods and then shipping cheap items back to their clients.

As planters cleared more acres to grow tobacco, the demand for field workers grew, too. Virginians first used British and African indentured servants to work the tobacco fields. An indentured servant worked in exchange for the cost of travel to America. Indentured men and women worked long hours grubbing in the tobacco fields. Cruel masters and mistresses often mistreated them. But after about seven years of labor the indentured servant earned his or her freedom.

By the 1670s African slaves carried more of the work burden. White Virginians viewed slavery as an economic bargain. An enslaved human being, once purchased, never gained his or her freedom but worked for life. A slave, like any piece of property, could be sold for quick cash or rented to another farm. Unlike indentured servants, who had some rights in court, a slave had no rights or protection. And a slave owner could acquire more slaves without any expense since a slave woman's child was also enslaved.

In young George Washington's world, Virginia's work and wealth depended on enslaved human beings. Gus Washington owned 20 slaves at Ferry Farm. Every day George saw African men and women planting, hoeing, and harvesting under the hot sun. Other enslaved people worked as house servants, washing clothes, cooking, or tending farm animals. For George, the enslaved workers living at Ferry Farm belonged to his father just like the looking glass in the hall.

Family Matters

George greeted the return of Lawrence and Austin from England with great excitement. About 20 years old, dark-haired Lawrence especially captivated his younger brother. Everyone thought George, like his father and older brothers, would enroll at Appleby School in England to finish his education. In the meantime, George probably did lessons at home with his father or a traveling teacher. He may also have attended a neighborhood school.

The year George turned eight Lawrence joined an American regiment in the British

Lawrence Washington.

army. With England and Spain at war, Lawrence prepared to sail with 400 Virginians under British admiral Edward Vernon to the Caribbean. The sight of his brother–now Captain Washington!–in his scarlet uniform with shining brass buttons thrilled George, who never lost his love for military finery.

Months later Lawrence returned home and spoke with great admiration of Admiral Vernon. But he talked bitterly about the British officers who looked down on colonial troops. They kept the Virginians crammed aboard ships to die of disease. George, feeling anger for Lawrence, tucked his brother's bitterness away into his memories.

Then, on April 12, 1743, George Washington's life changed. His father died a few months after George's 11th birthday. With Gus's death, all hopes for George attending school in England ended. In fact, his chance for a successful future lay under a cloud. Gus divided his several farms and 49 slaves among his children. Lawrence, the oldest son, received Little Hunting Creek plantation and the iron mines. Austin received the Popes Creek farm, George's birthplace. Gus left Ferry Farm, 10 slaves, and a few small lots in Fredericksburg to George. Mary would oversee George's property until he came of age. Overnight George became the man of the house, the oldest of Mary's five children at Ferry Farm.

As Gus had done after Jane died, most men and women in colonial America remarried soon after the death of a spouse. People believed both a man and a woman were required to raise children and run a farm and home smoothly. But Mary Washington did not remarry. With Gus gone, tension appeared between George and his mother.

Stubborn and strong-willed, Mary often seemed most worried about herself. How would George's actions affect her? George rarely won his mother's approval. He felt smothered. As much as possible he fled Ferry Farm to visit Lawrence and Austin.

Education of Many Sorts

Without the money for an English education, George had to pursue more practical forms of schooling. Instead of Latin, Greek, or philosophy, George studied geography, math, and geometry, the skills necessary for accounting and land surveying. His handwriting and math diagrams show great care. He spent time doing them well, adding touches of artistic flair. All his life George loved beauty in things great and small; he loved careful details and planning. George Washington's formal schooling ended when he was 14 or 15. His greatest teacher would be his life experiences.

Young Washington also studied good manners as a way to better himself in society.

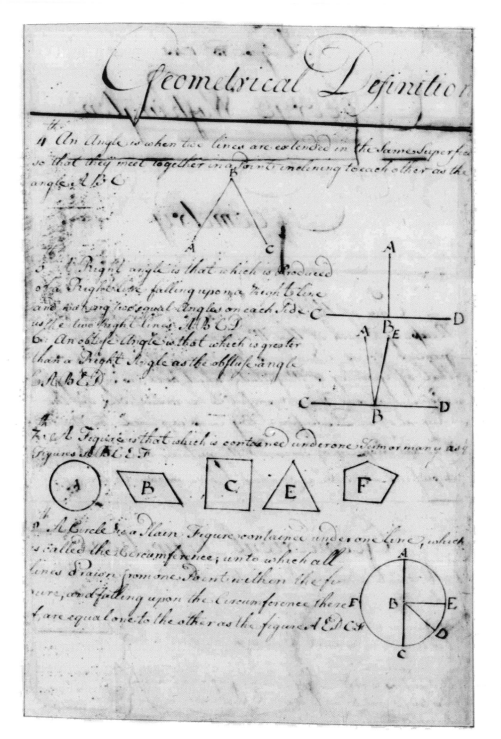

Geometrical Definition

4 An Angle is when two lines are extended in the same superfice so that they meet together in a point inclining to each other as the angle ABC

5 A Right angle is that which is produced of a Right line falling upon a Right line and making two equal angles on each side as the two Right lines ABCD

6 An obtuse angle is that which is greater than a Right angle as the obtuse angle ABED

7 A Figure is that which is contained under one Term or many as the figures ABCEF

8 A Circle is a Plain Figure contained under one line, which is called the Circumference; unto which all lines drawn from one Point within the figure, and falling upon the Circumference there of, are equal one to the other as the figure AEDCA

George carefully prepared his geometry lesson on this page of his school copy book.
Library of Congress

Young Washington's Rules for Good Behavior

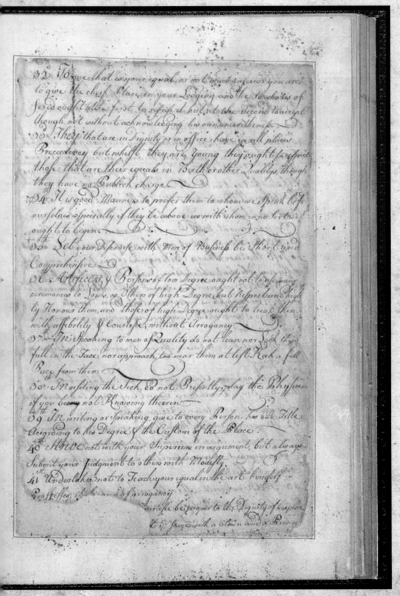

This is a page from George Washington's "Rules of Civility," written in his own hand. Library of Congress

A sampling from George Washington's "Rules of Civility and Decent Behavior in Company and Conversation."

4th: "In the presence of others sing not to yourself with a humming noise, nor drum with your fingers or feet."

37th: "In speaking to men of quality, do not lean nor look them full in the face, nor approach too near them, at least keep a full pace from them."

53rd: "Run not in the streets; neither go too slowly nor with mouth open; go not shaking your arms; kick not the earth with your feet. Go not upon the toes nor in a dancing fashion."

90th: "Being set at meat [eating], scratch not; neither spit, cough, or blow your nose, except there's a necessity for it."

Without a father, George needed all the help he could get. Fine manners might earn him attention and favor from "men of quality" who could shape his future.

When he was 14 George copied 110 rules of civility and good manners from a book first published for French aristocrats. George's list included rules for table manners, dress, and showing respect to others. The list carried reminders on how to behave with his "betters," with his "equals," and with "inferior" people. All the rules stressed the effect his behavior had on the feelings of others.

Teenage George carefully tracked every penny he spent. George generously lent small sums to friends. He bought a translation of Roman general Julius Caesar's *Commentaries.* George also enjoyed card games, like loo and whist, and like many Virginians he enjoyed gambling on card and dice games.

Every Virginia gentleman needed dancing skills; dancing was one of the colony's main social pastimes. So George paid for dancing lessons. Dancing masters were not shy about whacking their students with a heavy cane for blundering through a dance. George mastered the intricate steps of formal dances, like minuets, but he especially liked lively "country" dances like square dances and reels performed by couples facing each other in two lines. At one point he wrote to Lawrence that he could not get to an "assembly," or ball, because he couldn't afford to buy feed for his horse.

A Book of Good Manners

Books on manners played an important role in educating young people in colonial America. These rules helped George grow into the man he wanted to be: a polite member of Virginia's upper class—a man of quality. Many rules from Washington's time still apply today. What do you want to live up to? What rules would you write to create a better, more polite world?

Materials

Pencil

Sheets plain school paper

Unlined heavy paper from an office supply store (look for 24-weight paper made with cotton)

Ruler

Colored pens

2 8½-by-11-inch sheets poster board

2 paint colors (you can match the pen, ribbon, and paint colors)

Shallow foil pan

Piece of sponge

Hole punch

3 strips narrow ribbon (about 10 inches long) in any color

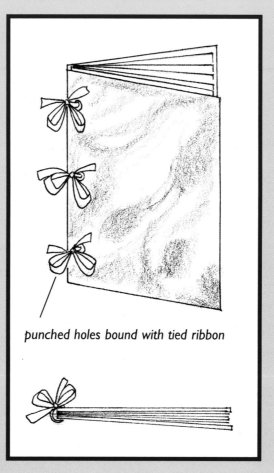

punched holes bound with tied ribbon

Brainstorm your ideas and write them on the school paper. When you're finished, take a fresh sheet of the heavy paper. Like in colonial days, use a ruler and lightly pencil in your lines. Number your rules and write them in pen using your fanciest handwriting. Use as many sheets of paper as you need.

Create a title for your book like Washington's "Rules of Civility and Decent Behavior in Company and Conversation." The two sheets of poster board will be your book cover.

Pour one of the paint colors into a shallow foil pan. Dip the sponge in the paint then dab the color onto the poster board. Let the paint dry. Do the same thing with the second color, letting some of the first color show through. Let dry. Punch three holes into the side of your papers and the poster board covers. Slip a piece of ribbon through each hole and tie to create a book.

The Ohio Company

In 1747 a group of Virginians formed the Ohio Company. They hoped to grow rich by acquiring western lands along the Ohio River and selling them to settlers. Members included Lawrence Washington, William Fairfax, Robert Dinwiddie (Virginia's lieutenant governor), and men in London. In 1749 the British king granted the Ohio Company 500,000 western acres. In exchange, the company should build a British fort in the Ohio River Valley and encourage 200 families to move west. The Ohio Company planned to use the fort as a trading post for valuable furs supplied by Native Americans. There was one problem, however. The king of France claimed the same lands in the Ohio River Valley.

George also grew concerned about his dress and appearance. Virginians judged a man on the cleanliness and quality of his clothes. Most people dressed in similar fashions, but people of quality dressed in better fabrics more carefully cut, tailored, and sewn. For one visit, George packed a razor, nine shirts, six linen handkerchiefs, and four neck bands.

The Fairfax Family

As George stretched his wings, Lawrence Washington was rising in Virginia society. He aimed to carry his little brother along with him. Lawrence bought more land and renamed the Little Hunting Creek house "Mount Vernon" in honor of Admiral Vernon. He'd been elected to the Virginia House of Burgesses and served as the adjutant general, which means he was in charge of training Virginia's volunteer militias. In 1743 Lawrence married a Mount Vernon neighbor, Anne Fairfax. The Fairfax family belonged to an influential, wealthy English clan. Anne's father, William, oversaw five million acres of Virginia lands granted to his family in 1649. The lands belonged to William's cousin Thomas, the Sixth Lord Fairfax.

When George was 14 Lawrence rushed a note to him at Ferry Farm. George must meet William Fairfax in Fredericksburg to discuss George's future. Fairfax could secure George a job as midshipman on the vessel of Captain Green of the Royal Navy. This was a big step for any young man. Mary Washington sought advice and considered the offer for a year before refusing.

Often at Mount Vernon, George became a regular visitor at the Fairfax home, Belvoir. The mansion's beauty and grandeur awed the teenager. Belvoir's nine rooms included two fully furnished sitting rooms, and unlike at Ferry Farm, there wasn't a bedstead in sight! Belvoir's dining room boasted gleaming mahogany furniture, silver, and paintings worth 10 times the furnishings in Ferry Farm's hall. The Fairfax home opened a grand new world for George.

William Fairfax was not only wealthy but also a man of influence, a member of the king's council in Virginia. As a young man without a father, and not very well educated, George needed influential friends to get ahead. Fairfax recognized George's eagerness to learn, and applauded the young man's determination to make his way in the world. Even as a teenager George's energy, passion, and strength shone through. When he made friends with William Fairfax's son, serious and timid George William, it was Washington—six years younger—who became the leader of the two.

William Fairfax's attitudes impressed George. A man's greatest achievement, William Fairfax believed, was to win the respect of his countrymen. George could also

Dance the Minuet

George Washington loved dancing, a popular pastime and important social skill in colonial Virginia. Dancing masters drilled children in this necessary social grace; dancing manuals were also studied. The minuet was a slow, formal, elegant dance between a gentleman and a lady. There are many variations to this dance—here is a simple minuet to try!

Materials

18th century music by composers such as
    Handel, Bach, Mozart, or Haydn
Partner

First perform the courtesies: ladies curtsey and gentlemen bow. Curtsey by holding your dress out to the sides, placing one foot slightly behind the other, and bending your knees. Keep your back straight, your eyes lowered modestly. Gentlemen bow by bending slightly forward at the waist, left leg

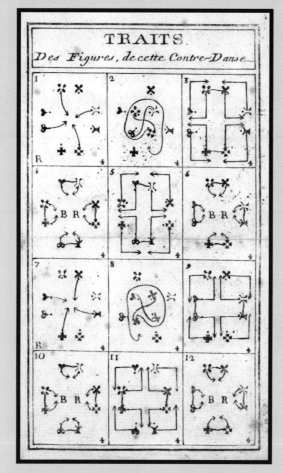

Dance steps and movements illustrated in a French dancing manual from the 1780s.

Library of Congress LC-DIG-ppmsca-02564

back and right leg slightly forward, arms out to the side. When you dance, stand tall. Make eye contact with your partner. Everyone is watching to see how elegantly you carry yourself.

Stand to one side of your partner and face forward. The lady puts her raised left hand on the gentleman's right hand. Step forward with your right leg straight and toes pointed, the left leg slightly bent. Take 3 small steps: right foot, left foot, right foot. Point the left toe in front of you and tap it 3 times against the floor. Repeat this dance sequence 3 times, switching your starting leg each time. Then face your partner, and bow and curtsey.

Now, turn in the opposite direction with the lady's right hand touching the gentleman's left hand. Repeat steps from above until the music stops. Finish with more courtesies.

Lord Thomas Fairfax.

see that the more land a man owned the greater his base for wealth and power.

In the summer of 1746 Belvoir hummed with excitement. Lord Fairfax himself, towing trunks of fine clothes and his own foxhounds, arrived in Virginia. Thomas Fairfax was the first member of the British aristocracy George Washington ever met. If the short, rather chubby lord was not George's idea of a dashing nobleman, he kept quiet. Lord Fairfax disliked women—he'd been jilted by a runaway bride—and loved foxhunting. The sport showed off George's superb horse skills. Never tiring, he galloped across fields and flew over fences, winning approval from the grumpy English lord.

William Fairfax included 16-year-old George in a surveying party sent over the Blue Ridge Mountains to lay out farm-sized lots of Fairfax lands. George spent 31 days in March and April 1748 tramping through the West. He kept a journal of his first great adventure. The wild beauty, the mountains, and the limitless forests of towering trees filled his senses. The group slept under the stars or shared the hospitality of frontier families in one-room cabins. One night George lay down on a bed of matted straw covered by "one threadbare blanket, with double its weight of vermin, such as lice, fleas, etc."

The survey team swam their horses across the rushing Potomac, the river swollen with melted mountain snows. One night they met a group of Native Americans who entertained the surveying party with drumming and dancing. The group got lost at least once in the mountains. Through pouring rain they paddled their canoes 40 miles in one day. George hunted wild turkeys and encountered a rattlesnake. He kept field notes for the professional surveyor, studied the man's methods, and practiced with surveying tools that had belonged to his father. The vast, powerful wilderness tugged at George's soul, creating a lifelong bond with the West.

George William Fairfax and Lawrence served together in the House of Burgesses during the winter of 1748–49. When George William returned to Belvoir he brought his 18-year-old bride, Sally. Like George William, Sally Fairfax came from an old and wealthy Virginia family. The bride's flashing dark eyes, dark curls, and flirtatious personality soon captured George Washington. At some point, poor George fell in love with Sally Fairfax, his friend's wife.

Native Americans entertain Washington and George William Fairfax, 1748.

Northwind Picture Archives

The Young Surveyor

In 1749, with a good word from William Fairfax, Virginia's government appointed 17-year-old George an official county surveyor. As a sworn official George measured the exact size of land lots, creating important records. He also mapped and divided large tracts of land into individual lots. The job paid well, and as a professional man, George earned respect.

George liked surveying. It matched his artistic talents, his eye for planning and detail. George proved a hard worker and a busy one. Young and strong, he tackled difficult surveying journeys, crossing the Blue Ridge again in

Make a Compass

One of George Washington's most valuable surveyor's tools was his compass. The compass let him know what direction he was facing. The magnetized arrows on the compass turned to the earth's closest magnetic point, in this case the North Pole. Most compasses had covered brass or wood cases to protect the instrument.

Materials

Bowl
Water
Bar magnet
Sewing needle
2-inch-wide square of paper

Fill the bowl with water and set it on a table. Take the magnet and stroke it— each stroke going the same direction— with the duller end of the sewing needle, being careful not to stick yourself. Make at least ten strokes. This lines up electrons inside the needle, turning it into a magnet. Place the sheet of paper to float on top of the water. Place the needle on top of the paper.

Give the paper a tap with your finger. When the paper stops slowly turning, your needle should be pointed north. Keep the magnet and other metal objects at least 2 feet away while you are testing your compass. If you have a real compass, test how well your needle compass has worked.

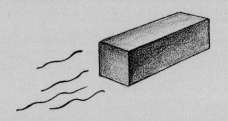

1750 to lay out 47 tracts of land. By the end of the year he'd earned enough to invest money in 1,459 acres of land on Bullskin Creek, a tributary of the Shenandoah River. All of 18, George felt himself on the path to success.

George also spent time at Ferry Farm visiting his younger siblings and mother. One morning he stripped off his clothes, dropped them on the river bank, and dove into the Rappahannock for a swim. When he climbed out of the water, his clothes had vanished, swiped by two servant girls!

Caring for Lawrence

One dark cloud shadowed George's life. For over a year Lawrence had been plagued by a racking cough. George and his brother traveled to Warm Springs (near present day Berkeley Springs, West Virginia) in hopes of improving Lawrence's health. Suffering people drank from the bubbling waters and bathed in the springs. But George worried the seeping chill would not help Lawrence. "The afternoon's sun is hid by four o'clock," he wrote, "and the fog hangs over us till nine or ten, which occasion great damp mornings, and evenings to be cool."

In September 1751 the brothers tried a warmer climate. They sailed to Barbados in the Caribbean. The voyage was George's first and only time at sea. He loved the island's exotic green beauty, bright blossoms, and tangy breezes swept in from the sea. For exercise the brothers rode horses, leaving at dawn to escape the afternoon heat. They ventured out again in the evenings. One night George attended a play. The actors striding about the stage, the music, the flickering lights, and the fashionably dressed audience thrilled George. For the rest of his life Washington seldom missed a chance to attend the theater.

But Lawrence weakened, his body doubled over with painful bouts of coughing. To make matters worse, George caught smallpox. With Lawrence nursing him, George recovered from the deadly disease, which left him scarred by a few slight pockmarks on his nose. But this bout with smallpox protected George from catching the disease again.

In years to come George never mentioned the trip to Barbados in his writings. Watching his beloved brother dying, probably of tuberculosis, was too painful. Lawrence sailed on to try the climate in Bermuda, but George returned to Virginia and his surveying job in January 1752.

Growing Pains

When the average height of a man was five feet, seven inches, George had grown into an athletic young man about six feet, two inches tall. He radiated a sense of strength and power.

George Washington began working at age 17 as a land surveyor.
Library of Congress, LC-USZ62-74107

Washington's Poetry

George may have been a bit awkward around girls as a teenager but that didn't stop him from writing love poems. From his lovelorn pen George wrote:

*Oh, ye Gods, why should my poor resist-
    less heart
Stand to oppose thy might and power
At last surrender to Cupid's feather'd
    dart . . .*

Luckily, George did not seek a career in poetry.

He stood out across a room with his height and red-brown hair pulled neatly back into a "queue," or ponytail. One man described George's blue-gray eyes as "penetrating." When talking with someone, "he looks you full in the face." But he was a bit awkward, with his large hands and feet. Shy, proud, and quiet, George usually thought carefully before he spoke. He did not easily flirt with girls or make chitchat.

Upper-class Virginians based marriage more on money matters than love. Parents often arranged a son or daughter's marriage. In May 1752 George proposed marriage to 16-year-old Betsy Fauntleroy, daughter of a wealthy Virginian. Twice, Betsy turned him down. The Fauntleroys would not accept him into their upper-crust world.

And even though George was now an adult, Mary refused to turn over control of Ferry Farm, his inheritance from his father. In fact, though she had her own money and property, Mary refused to move for another 20 years!

Then, in July 1752, Lawrence died. He left his grieving brother several parcels of land. Lawrence also left Mount Vernon to George, *if* George outlived Lawrence's widow, Anne, and the couple's baby girl. Six months after Lawrence's death Anne remarried and moved to her new husband's home. George rented Mount Vernon from Anne for 15,000 pounds of tobacco a year. Often lonely and depressed, he visited Belvoir to cheer himself up.

George continued surveying. He widened his circle of influential friends by joining the Masonic Lodge in Fredericksburg. George also applied to Lieutenant Governor Robert Dinwiddie for Lawrence's post as adjutant general of Virginia. It was a nervy move for a 20-year-old with no military experience! Yet George wanted the job and believed he could train the colony's volunteer militia soldiers.

Determined, George campaigned for the post. He visited government officials and impressed the men with his manners, charm, and ambition. Friends like William Fairfax also spoke on George's behalf. Dinwiddie divided the colony into four military districts. He gave George the rank of major, a small salary, and appointed him adjutant of the smallest district.

At 20 George Washington was a landowner and a successful surveyor, and now he'd added a military title to his list of accomplishments. He soon stepped from teenage awkwardness into the boots of a young man who danced gracefully and rode a horse as well as—if not better than—anyone in Virginia. A good life seemed to be at George's fingertips. Instead, he chose to test himself again in the western wilderness.

(opposite page) George dances with Sally Fairfax at Belvoir.

Northwind Picture Archives

2

"I Heard the Bullets Whistle"

umors rumbled into Williamsburg. Great Britain's long-time enemy in Europe and rival in North America—France—stirred in the north. The French had moved down from Canada, pressing south of Lake Erie onto lands also claimed by the British king in the Ohio River Valley. In 1753 King George II asked Virginia's lieutenant governor, Robert Dinwiddie, to send an "emissary," or agent, to the French. The emissary should peacefully, but sternly, order the French to leave British lands. This emissary should also woo Native Americans toward the British side.

Whose Land Is It?

France controlled Canada and the Great Lakes in the north and the Louisiana Territory in the south. The Ohio River Valley and its trade networks linked France's two territories. The British also claimed the Ohio country. Native Americans lived on those lands and traded with both European nations.

For years the tribes had tipped the balance of power toward either France or Great Britain, depending on what best served Indian interests. Many tribes depended on European trade goods like fabric, guns, kettles, knives, and axes, and spent much of their time hunting and trapping for valuable pelts to trade.

Tribes like the Mingo, Shawnee, Delaware, and Miami lived in the Ohio country. The influence of the powerful Iroquois nations also stretched to the region. The members of the Iroquois confederacy—the Mohawk, Oneida, Onondaga, Cayuga, Seneca, and Tuscarora—usually leaned toward Great Britain. As tensions grew between France and Great Britain, Indian people had to decide which European power they stood to gain the most from.

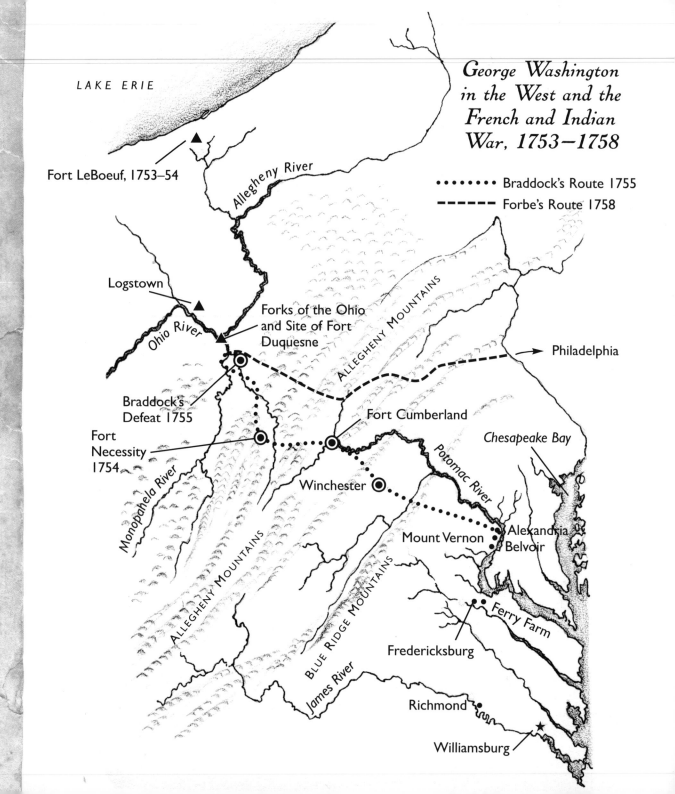

George Washington in the West and the French and Indian War, 1753–1758

•••••• Braddock's Route 1755
––––– Forbe's Route 1758

LAKE ERIE

Fort LeBoeuf, 1753–54

Allegheny River

Logstown

Ohio River

Forks of the Ohio and Site of Fort Duquesne

ALLEGHENY MOUNTAINS

Philadelphia

Braddock's Defeat 1755

Fort Necessity 1754

Fort Cumberland

Chesapeake Bay

Monopahela River

Winchester

Potomac River

Mount Vernon

Alexandria

Belvoir

ALLEGHENY MOUNTAINS

BLUE RIDGE MOUNTAINS

Ferry Farm

Fredericksburg

James River

Richmond

Williamsburg

George Washington in the West, 1753–58

George Washington, eager to prove himself and win recognition, volunteered for the job. Dinwiddie accepted him. Washington was only 21 and lacked diplomatic skills. But he had wilderness experience and was young and strong enough to make the rough journey—over 1,000 miles there and back.

Six others accompanied Washington, including Jacob van Braam, a Dutchman and French interpreter, and Christopher Gist, a fur trader who acted as guide. The small group set off on October 31, 1753. Washington carried a letter from Dinwiddie warning the French to leave the Ohio country.

From the start an icy rain pelted Washington's party. Snow already blanketed the mountains. Washington decided to push ahead and let the pack animals catch up. He had to reach the Forks of the Ohio as soon as possible. At this triangle of land, the Monongahela River and Allegheny River flowed together to form the Ohio River (the site of present-day Pittsburgh, Pennsylvania). Two days of scouting around the Forks revealed no French presence. Washington realized a large fort built here could control thousands of miles of wilderness. But who would build a fort here first, Great Britain or France?

Seneca leader Tanacharison, or Half King.

The expedition pushed ahead to Logstown, a Native American center for trade and diplomacy. Washington handed out strings of wampum beads and tobacco as a gesture of goodwill. He met with a Seneca leader named Tanacharison, called Half King by the English.

Half King represented the powerful Iroquois with the Ohio tribes. Washington scribbled notes as Half King repeated what he'd recently told the French:

Both you and the English are white, we live in a Country between; . . . the Great Being above allowed it to be a place of residence to us . . . ; So Fathers, I desire you to withdraw, as I have done our brothers the English; . . . I lay this down as a Trial for both, to see which will have the greatest Regard to it, and that Side we will stand by.

Washington asked the Logstown chiefs for some young men to guide them, hunt for

23

Follow the Tracks

Washington hired Native American scouts to track and hunt for him. A skilled tracker read forests, meadows, and streams for signs of animal life. Foods an animal left behind offered clues; gnawed nuts meant a squirrel. Were there teeth marks or claw marks on a tree branch? Even the animal's droppings told the hunter what creature had passed by. Most telling were the animal's footprints as it walked, bounded, hopped, or ran. A hunter could tell how fast the animal moved by the distance between its prints.

Materials

Notebook or journal
Pencil or pen

Walk in the park on a snowy or damp day, or just look outside your door, and see if you can recognize signs that an animal has been there. Keep track of what you find in a nature journal. Draw and measure the tracks. Can you identify the animal that made them?

Record anything else you observe. Where do the tracks lead? Are there more than one species in the same area? Could one animal have been chasing another? Have fun!

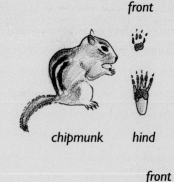

front

chipmunk   hind

front

rabbit   hind   squirrel   front   hind   white-tailed deer   front   hind

front

striped skunk   hind   raccoon   front   hind   opossum   front   hind

them, and help protect them "against those French Indians who have taken up the hatchet against us." The French Indians were those Native Americans who supported the French at the time. Only Half King and a few elderly chiefs, plus one hunter to provide meat, joined Washington.

Washington reached Fort LeBoeuf (near Lake Erie and present-day Waterford, Pennsylvania) on December 11, soaked to the bone and caked with mud. The next day he changed into his militia officer's uniform and in the name of the governor of Virginia and King George II, solemnly handed over his letter to the fort commander, Legardeur de St. Pierre.

As the French discussed the letter Washington wandered around Fort LeBoeuf making notes. He counted over 200 canoes ready to launch toward the Forks of the Ohio. St. Pierre showed Washington great courtesy, but his answer to Dinwiddie's letter was simple: "As to the summons you send me to retire, I do not think myself obliged to obey it."

The journey back to Williamsburg became a winter nightmare. Glittering ice encased bushes, brambles, and trees. Horses and men staggered through drifts of ice-crusted snow. The thirsty men tried to suck bits of ice for water, but it was so bitterly cold it burned their mouths. Along the way Washington changed to "Indian dress," leather leggings and a knee-length belted coat. George decided to take Gist, his guide, and push ahead of the

Washington's winter journey through the wilderness after delivering a warning to the French.

25

exhausted packhorses. He had to warn Din-widdie that a French invasion of the Ohio country seemed likely.

The two men set off through the snow, their faces red with cold, their vaporous breath hanging in the air. They stumbled into a "party of French Indians, who had lain in Wait for us. One of them fired at Mr. Gist or me, not 15 steps [ahead] but fortunately missed," wrote Washington. He and Gist stopped only to catch their breath and their bearings.

Two days later they reached the Allegheny River. Washington had hoped to find a smooth frozen surface to cross. Instead the Allegheny roared and churned with huge chunks of ice. The two men built a raft and, armed with long poles, tried to push their way across. Hunks of ice smashed into the raft, knocking Washington's pole. He tumbled into the freezing waters. Water-soaked clothes pulled his body down. "I fortunately saved myself by catching hold of one of the Raft Logs," he wrote. With a mighty effort he heaved himself back onto the raft. His clothes froze against his skin. The raft could not reach either shore. As darkness closed in, Washington and Gist guided the raft to a small island, where they tried to sleep. The next morning the Allegheny had frozen solid! They walked across to the far shore.

Washington arrived in Williamsburg on January 16, 1754, and reported to Dinwiddie. Within days the lieutenant governor published Washington's report of the expedition, hoping

Washington and Gist try to cross the Allegheny River on a raft.

to publicize the danger of French plans for the Ohio country.

The Virginia assembly voted to pay Washington 50 pounds sterling for his journey—which barely covered his expenses. "I was employed," he wrote, "to go on a journey in the winter (when I believe few or none would have undertaken it), and what did I get by it? My expenses borne." This would not be the last time George felt snubbed and overlooked.

Setting a Match to War

Dinwiddie convinced the Virginia legislature to raise 300 men to build a fort at the Forks of the Ohio. He offered Washington command of the new expedition. Washington, however, turned him down, fearing "it is a charge too great for my youth and inexperience." He would be happy, however, to serve as second in command and learn on the job. Dinwiddie named Joshua Fry the commander.

A small force forged ahead to begin building the fort. They reported back that rumors flew everywhere of a large French invasion. By mid-March 1754 Dinwiddie ordered Washington "to march whatever soldiers you have enlisted immediately to the Ohio." Washington gathered what supplies, horses, and wagons he could. On April 2 he left with 159 men. Joshua Fry would follow as soon as possible with the rest of the 300 men.

Washington, the 22-year-old with no military experience, was on his own.

Washington's force began carving a road for the supply wagons through the wilderness. The soldiers hacked away brush, brambles, and trees. Then, on April 20, Washington learned the new fort, barely even built, had been captured by a force of 1,000 French soldiers and their Indian allies.

Washington established a camp at the Great Meadows, an open grassy area with a ribbon of winding stream in southwestern Pennsylvania. He continued work on the wilderness road and sent messages to the governors of Virginia and Pennsylvania asking for more aid. Almost daily rumors warned Washington that the French marched to attack him. A French fort, named Fort Duquesne, rose rapidly on the triangle of land at the Forks of the Ohio.

By nightfall on May 27, 1754, a curtain of rain pelted the camp, soaking tents and chilling the Virginia volunteer soldiers. At about 8:00 P.M. an Indian messenger burst into camp with news from Half King. Seneca scouts had spotted a party of French soldiers nearby. Washington sprang into action. He secured his camp then gathered 40 men and marched into the pitch-dark forest to meet Half King, camped six miles away.

After a brief council of war, Washington and Half King decided to strike the French camp. The early-morning skirmish, Washington's first battle, ended quickly. Ten French

soldiers were killed; among them was the French commander, Joseph Coulon de Villiers, Sieur de Jumonville. One man escaped to run barefoot through 60 miles of forest to Fort Duquesne.

Washington did not believe French protests that they were a peaceful diplomatic mission sent to warn the English out of the Ohio River Valley. Why, Washington demanded, had a diplomatic mission come in secrecy, hidden in a ravine for days, and not sought him out to talk? In fact, Washington's men discovered a second set of papers in the French camp showing that Jumonville had spied on the English and reported back to French commanders. Washington ordered the surviving French soldiers marched to Winchester.

After the skirmish George wrote to his brother John about his small victory: "I can with truth assure you, I heard the bullets whistle, and believe me there is something charming in the sound." Years later when asked about this comment Washington replied that if he'd written such words, "I must have been very young."

Fort Necessity

Back at the Great Meadows Washington ordered trees felled and a circle of logs dug into the ground. He named the hastily built structure Fort Necessity. Unimpressed, Half

A replica of Fort Necessity stands in the Great Meadows. French and Indian forces attacked Washington here on July 3, 1754. Courtesy of Tom Ratterman

King called it "that little thing in the meadows." Washington dashed off a letter to Dinwiddie. He expected a French attack any moment and knew he'd be outnumbered. But he promised the Virginians would do "our duty in fighting as long [as] there was any possibility of hope." Then word reached camp that Joshua Fry had died. Washington was promoted to colonel of the Virginia Regiment.

Reinforcements arrived. These colonial troops, led by Captain James Mackay, had been made part of the British regular army. While Mackay and Washington bristled over who was in charge they heard that a huge French force, 800 soldiers and 400 Indians, was headed toward the Great Meadows.

Washington pulled the road crews back to the fort. He dug trenches and built earthworks around Fort Necessity. Half King complained that Washington ignored his advice and insulted the Indians by telling them how to fight. Native Americans preferred to strike by ambush and not risk their warriors in a direct, open attack the way Europeans fought. With word of the French approach the Native Americans packed their belongings and melted into the forest.

Early in the morning on July 3, 1754, French troops and their Indian allies attacked Fort Necessity. They hid in the brush and forest surrounding the open meadow, firing from "every little rising, tree, stump, stone, and bush" into the fort. The fight lasted for hours. Then a wall of rain enveloped the Great Meadows. The trenches filled with knee-deep water turned red with blood. The roof over the powder magazine leaked, ruining the gunpowder. Again and again Washington rallied his troops, stepping over fallen soldiers and slipping on grass drenched with rain and blood. As darkness fell, the situation could not get much worse. More than 100 of his men lay dead, dying, or wounded.

And then the French signaled they were willing to discuss terms for Washington's surrender. Washington sent Jacob van Braam, the interpreter, across the meadow to meet the French commander, Louis Coulon de Villiers. Several times van Braam reported back to Washington and returned to the French with more questions. Each time, de Villiers agreed to Washington's changes without a word of protest.

At last van Braam carried back incredible news–if the British surrendered, they could simply go home. Thrilled and relieved, Washington agreed. He was too young and inexperienced to wonder why the French offered such generous terms of surrender. He may not even have known that the French commander was the brother of Jumonville, killed at the French camp in the ravine.

By candlelight, with the ink running in the rain, van Braam and Washington pored over the surrender agreement. Then Washington penned his signature to the paper. Due to poor translation, eagerness, or exhaustion, Washington did not understand certain passages in the surrender paper. The French commander had carefully worded parts of the document. In signing, Washington admitted the French had only attacked him to avenge Washington's secret murder of the French diplomat, Jumonville.

On July 4, with drummers beating a march, the British left Fort Necessity with their flags flying. Seventy wounded rode in wagons or on the backs of their fellow soldiers. About three miles away they stopped and camped, too exhausted to continue. Washington galloped ahead to report to Dinwiddie.

Fallout from Washington's actions rippled far and wide. His defeat at Fort Necessity showed British weakness to the Native Ameri-cans. The majority of Indians decided to stay neutral or help the French. Before long the entire British frontier was under Indian attack. One British Indian agent noted, "There was never the like seen how quick the [Indian] nations turned after Colonel Washington's defeat." And in Europe, Washington's actions embarrassed Great Britain as France loudly condemned the murder of a French diplomat.

Washington had desperately hoped to win a lifetime commission in the regular British army. If a commissioned officer retired due to age or injury he received half pay for life. If a man wanted to change careers he could even sell his commission for thousands of pounds sterling. And Washington hated that American officers were treated as inferiors and paid less than British regular soldiers. Why "the lives of His Majesty's subjects in Virginia should be of less value" he did not know. Did he recall Lawrence's bitterness all those years ago?

He hoped his Virginia Regiment would be blended into the regular British army, and of course Washington would become a regular colonel at age 22! Washington, however, was fooling himself. A valuable commission like this would go to a young man of aristocratic birth. And British military men scoffed at the idea of bumbling colonial officers standing on the same level as officers in the regular British army. The British ambassador to France wrote, "Washington and many such may have courage and resolution, but they have no knowledge or experience . . . there can be no dependence on them."

Instead, the government broke the Virginia regiment up. No colonist would be given a commission higher than captain. Washington's rank plunged from colonel to captain–a demotion! And he would always be under a regular British officer, even one with a rank lower than his own. The decision came as a slap in the face to the ambitious young man. Disappointed and obeying "the call of honor," Washington resigned from the army.

The Braddock Campaign

If the military didn't want him, George would farm. Mary Washington would not budge from Ferry Farm, so George retired to Mount Vernon. Lawrence's little girl, Sarah, had died. Now George was Anne's heir to the Mount Vernon estate.

George had barely settled into Mount Vernon in February 1755 when he heard news that British general Edward Braddock and two regiments of British troops had orders to capture Fort Duquesne. Washington rushed a letter to Braddock with congratulations. He watched British ships sail up the Potomac past Mount Vernon to Alexandria. Huge cannon and artillery wagons arrived, along with crates of guns, tents, and uniforms. Braddock wanted 200 wagons and 2,500 horses for his campaign.

The French and Indian War

Washington's battles in western Pennsylvania helped start a huge war. The French and Indian War (1754–63) fought in North American was part of a larger conflict called the Seven Years' War (1756–63). This war spread across Europe and even to India. It pitted France, Austria, Russia, Saxony, and Sweden against Great Britain, Prussia, Hanover, and Spain. In the end, Great Britain stood victorious and France lost its North American possessions.

Washington marveled at the sheer size of the camp. The Virginia militias couldn't compare with Braddock's professional, disciplined soldiers. They marched, drilled, and turned in rows of splendid scarlet coats and shining trim.

Braddock met Washington and invited him to join his "family" of young officers and aides. Washington eagerly accepted, hoping Braddock's influence and power could help him in the future, "if I find it worth pushing my fortune in the military way." But Braddock could not offer him a rank the young man thought suitable. Washington volunteered to serve as an unpaid aide without rank.

Braddock's force began building and improving a road toward Fort Duquesne. For Washington, the army crept at a turtle's pace. The British engineers halted "to level every mole hill and to erect bridges over every brook," he complained. Iroquois dropped into camp to check British progress. Washington advised Braddock that the Indians "are easily offended." But like other British officers, Braddock showed little respect for the Native Americans he wanted as allies. The Iroquois vanished into the forest, leaving the British to their own troubles.

As the days wore on Washington suffered headaches, fever, and dysentery, called the "bloody flux." Too weak to ride his horse, he traveled in a wagon. He advised Braddock to pick up the pace: take 1,200 chosen troops and about 30 cannon, and let horses carry the food and tents instead of the lumbering wagons. The rest of the force would follow.

Washington's health did not improve. Soon he could not even climb into a wagon and spent days confined to his tent. His illness forced him to stay behind with the slower force. They passed the Great Meadows and the burned ruins of Fort Necessity. They passed the ravine where Jumonville had died. On July 8 they caught up with Braddock's force two miles from the Monongahela River and 12 miles from Fort Duquesne.

Washington awoke the next morning shaking and aching from head to toe. But Washington believed Braddock would win a great victory that day and he couldn't miss out. He somehow climbed onto his horse's back for the first time in a month and joined the general.

An advance guard set out. Behind them the main force of 750 men splashed across the Monongahela and began climbing the bank on the far side. Up ahead the forest filled with cries and explosions of gunfire. "Forward!" urged Braddock. Suddenly, the advance guard of British troops appeared running back toward them! They crashed into the ranks, terror distorting their faces.

Confusion raced like electricity through the soldiers. Washington and the other officers shouted orders, trying to calm the men and gain control. Bullets raked through the British lines, fired by an enemy hidden in the forest.

The men panicked as comrades fell dead beside them. Officers toppled from their horses. Washington's horse crumpled beneath him. He grabbed a riderless animal and swung into the saddle. Waving his sword he urged the men to stand and fight. Fury filled his voice as the regular soldiers broke their lines, shooting aimlessly into the woods and into other British soldiers.

Washington's coat tugged sideways—he looked down and saw that a bullet had ripped through his uniform. Red-faced and hoarse from shouting he fought his way to Braddock. Washington offered to lead a party of colonial troops to fight the "enemy in their own way," hidden by the forest. Braddock refused, then fell, wounded.

Battle of the Monongahela, July 9, 1755. Washington had two horses shot out from under him.

Courtesy of the Mount Vernon Ladies' Association

General Edward Braddock arrived in 1755 to capture Fort Duquesne.

Washington buried Braddock in the road.

Washington's second horse tumbled to the ground. A bullet ripped the hat from his head. In the middle of this nightmare waves of sickness and fever swept over him. He climbed onto a third horse. Braddock, bleeding on the ground, agreed to use the colonial troops, but now it was too late. The men lifted Braddock into a cart. He told Washington to ride back 40 miles and bring up reinforcements to cover the retreat back to Virginia.

Barely able to stay in the saddle, Washington galloped through darkness past groaning, dying men. Sometimes he had to stop and crawl to find the road. The news had flown ahead of him with retreating soldiers. Washington headed back to Braddock. The general died near Fort Necessity. Washington buried Braddock in the road. Wagons rolled over the grave, disguising where the general's body lay.

Ill and weak, Washington returned to Mount Vernon. He blamed the defeat on the "dastardly behavior" of the British regular troops who panicked and fled. Washington's leadership and bravery at Braddock's defeat spread his name throughout the colonies.

The official British report, however, blamed colonials like Washington. The British troops marched to Philadelphia, leaving Virginia to fend for itself. New British strategy concentrated on attacking the French to the north in the Great Lakes. If successful, they'd cut off French supply routes to Fort Duquesne.

Frontier in Flames

British failure, including Washington's defeat at Fort Necessity, opened Virginia's frontier to Native American attacks. The Virginia legislature called on 23-year-old Washington to protect the frontier as commander in chief "of all forces now raised in the defense of His Majesty's Colony."

Mary Washington pressured George to refuse the commission. She worried about her son and believed his military service left him no time for her needs. "Honored Madam:" Washington wrote back, "If the command is pressed upon me by the general voice of the country . . . it would reflect . . . dishonor upon me to refuse it, and that, I am sure, must (or ought to) give you greater cause of uneasiness than my going."

Washington arrived at headquarters at Fort Cumberland, just over the Virginia border inside Maryland. Here he clashed with Captain John Dagworthy. Dagworthy claimed his rank of captain in the regular British army outranked Washington's commission as commander in chief of a colonial force. He ordered Washington's troops about and helped himself to Washington's hard-earned supplies. Seething at this treatment, Washington left Fort Cumberland and set up headquarters at Winchester in the Shenandoah Valley, 50 miles away from Dagworthy.

Mary Washington.

Library of Congress, LC-USZC4-7247

Washington's task proved impossible. The frontier was wide. Native Americans quickly hit isolated farms, then vanished. White survivors fled their burned homesteads and straggled into Winchester for protection. But Washington's force was too small to make any real difference. And Washington's complaints about lack of money, supplies, and soldiers were not winning friends back in Williamsburg. "I hope the affairs of the regiment are not in so bad a condition as represented here," Dinwiddie replied to one of Washington's letters. But Washington's hard-won experiences were turning him into a leader. His polite and easy manner won him the respect of his officers and soldiers. Washington was seldom rude and rarely swore. He shared his men's danger and hardships. His men appreciated that he rewarded a man based on his merit and bravery. He praised the regiment as a whole more than he praised any one man. It was the regiment, and pride in the regiment, that counted most.

Washington used a combination of inspiration, persuasion, and (when necessary) threats to lead his men. He insisted on strict military discipline, "the soul of an army," he called it. Soldiers who misbehaved or disobeyed orders were threatened, whipped, and in severe cases even hanged. But he pardoned most offenders.

The Big City

Washington protested his treatment at Fort Cumberland in letters to Dinwiddie and Massachusetts governor William Shirley, commander of British troops in North America. But that wasn't enough; he decided to plead his case to Shirley in person. In February 1756 he left for Boston, his first trip through settled areas of other colonies. He designed a new uniform for the occasion: a blue coat with scarlet trim, a waistcoat (vest) of scarlet with silver lace, blue breeches (pants), and silver lace upon his hat.

On his 24th birthday Washington visited Philadelphia, the largest city in the colonies. He gawked like a country boy, wandering streets jammed with people, carts, carriages, and animals. Philadelphia enticed with taverns, inns, shops bursting with goods, street stalls laden with food and treats.

Like a tourist, George spent freely at the tailors, hatters, and jewelers, and at a saddler. Then it was on to New York. He stayed with friends and visited a show called *Microcosm or the World in Miniature*. Clockworks moved sculptures, a circling heaven of stars, and mechanical dolls—it was so amazing George paid to go twice! He attended dances, lost money playing cards, and continued spending his cash.

In Boston, Washington interrupted his shopping to visit Governor Shirley. Shirley brushed aside Dagworthy's commission as not really in the regular British army. This meant George had command over Dagworthy. But Shirley refused to clear up the question of rank between British and colonial officers. And the governor ignored Washington's request for blending the Virginia regiment into the British military. Washington's money had flown from his pockets; for the trip back to Virginia he borrowed money. On the way home he wondered if he shouldn't once again resign.

Who to Blame?

Dinwiddie had tired of Washington's "unmannerly" complaints that the Virginia government failed to raise enough men and money. He ordered Washington to leave his headquarters at Winchester and return to Fort Cumberland, "the proper place for the Commanding Officer." Washington did so in December 1756. But he feared leaving Winchester's "poor, unhappy inhabitants . . . to . . . a merciless enemy." Most of all he feared blame would fall on him for "the murder of poor, innocent babes and helpless families."

George didn't know when to stop. He unwisely poured out his troubles to the Earl of Loudon, the new British military commander. Trying to shift blame away from himself,

Advertise Like a Colonist

Just like today, shop owners lured customers with signs showing off their wares or trade. Signs also showed what the shop did through pictures or their shape, for those customers who could not read. In a town like Williamsburg or Philadelphia George Washington saw signs for taverns and inns, wigmakers, shoemakers, bookbinders, milliners (makers of hats and ribbons), silversmiths, blacksmiths, apothecaries (druggists), coopers (barrel makers), chandlers (candle makers), cabinetmakers, tailors, saddlers, and many other trades.

Come up with a colonial trade and make a sign to advertise your business!

Adult supervision required

Materials

Piece of thick cardboard at least 20 inches tall and 15 inches wide (a 3-sided cardboard display board for school projects can be divided and used to make several activities)

Pencil

Craft knife with retractable blade

Paint in various colors

Paintbrush

Can of spray paint (optional)

Design the shape of your sign then draw it onto a piece of cardboard. With adult help, use the craft knife to cut out your sign. Paint the background of your sign with a brush or take the sign outside on the grass and give it a quick spray all over with a can of spray paint.

When the paint dries, draw a picture of your trade onto the painted cardboard. Using other paint colors, paint the design onto the sign.

George argued that his orders were unclear and confusing. Worst of all, "I am answerable for consequences and blamed without the privilege of defense." The Virginia Assembly, and the lack of men and supplies, hampered him. He worked tirelessly without reward. How could he serve in this situation without a loss of honor? The only solution to Virginia's frontier troubles, Washington urged Loudon, was the capture of Fort Duquesne. Washington got that off his chest, but heaping blame on royal officials did not score points with the aristocratic Lord Loudon.

Washington traveled to Philadephia to meet Loudon in late February 1757. At the same time he faced a new humiliation. France published a journal Washington had lost during the battle at Fort Necessity, dragging up the Jumonville Affair and Washington's defeat in the Great Meadow once again. Loudon kept Washington waiting for weeks, then ignored his complaints and dismissed him like a servant. There would be no attack on Fort Duquesne that year.

Washington's hopes lay smashed. For him there was no valuable commission, no honor. Hadn't his years of service earned him a regular commission? He'd even served Braddock without pay! Ambitious and sensitive about his honor and reputation, Washington felt stung. "We can't conceive," he wrote in March 1757, "that being Americans should deprive us of the benefits of British subjects." He continued his

mission to protect the frontier, trapped in a situation that seemed hopeless.

In August 1757 dysentery struck Washington again. By November he was nearly too weak to walk. Fort Cumberland's physician, Dr. James Craik, bled Washington often in hopes of ridding his body of disease. But nothing helped.

Finally George made the painful trip home to Mount Vernon, sick and depressed. "I now have no prospect left of preferment in a military way," he moaned. His body shook with fever and coughs, symptoms he remembered all too well in Lawrence. In March 1758 he dragged himself to Williamsburg. The doctor calmed George's fear—he was definitely not dying! Relief at the verdict put George on the road to recovery and a new military campaign.

Fort Duquesne

Great Britain's new prime minister, William Pitt, ordered a three-prong military campaign in North America, and one was against Fort Duquesne. His health restored, Washington lost no time contacting the man leading the Ohio campaign, Brigadier General John Forbes. The Virginia legislature offered Washington command of two Virginia regiments that would join Pennsylvanian and regular British troops. This time colonial officers could command regular soldiers of a lesser rank.

The people of Winchester beg Washington's help against Indian raids.

Northwind Picture Archives

Tie a Cravat

As a young man on the rise in colonial America it would have been important to George Washington that his clothes appeared fresh and crisp. Most clothing could not be washed since it was made of wool, which would shrink. People spot-cleaned outer garments or kept clothes perfumed with scented herbs. Only a person's "linen," their undergarments, like shifts (slips) for women and shirts for men, were washed regularly in a tub of hot, soapy water.

A clean linen neck cloth, or cravat, snowy white and pressed, marked a gentleman's wardrobe. So tie a fresh cravat around your neck and look like a gentleman.

Materials

Strip of muslin, linen, or cotton fabric
    5 inches wide and 5 feet long (fabric
    from an old white bedsheet can be used)
Lace trim (optional)
Mirror

Before you begin, if you want, sew lace trim along each short end for that real "man of quality" look. Now, stand in front of the mirror. Hang the fabric evenly around your neck with the ends hanging down. Wrap the ends around the front of your neck and drape them over your shoulders. Cross the ends loosely behind your neck and bring them around to the front again. Tuck the left end over and around the right end. Take the left end up and under the fabric wrapped around your neck. Pull the end down, straighten the cravat, and you are ready to go.

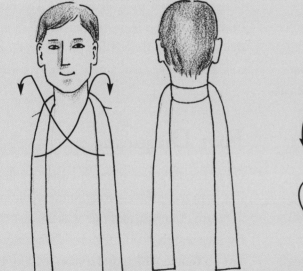

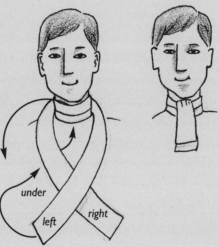

Washington could serve *and* save his honor! He hoped to get noticed "in some measure from the common run of provincial [colonial] officer, as I understand there will be a motley crew of us." Maybe his dream of a regular commission wasn't dead yet!

Washington passionately argued with Forbes over his strategy. Forbes planned to cut a new road across Pennsylvania to bring supplies from Philadelphia. Washington only saw how this hurt Virginia's economy and hopes for the Ohio Valley while helping Pennsylvania. He pushed to use the road Braddock's force had built, already improved to within six miles of Fort Duquesne. His dysentery returned and his spirits sank further. He wrote emotional letters expressing doom and gloom and blaming Forbes for opportunities wasted.

The expedition slogged through days of pounding rain. Wagons heavy with cannon and supplies sank into the mud. On November 12 word came that an enemy force was three miles away. Forbes sent Virginia soldiers to investigate. The rest of the army, waiting at camp, heard gunfire ahead.

Washington led a rescue mission of Virginia volunteers into the dark forest. As the party advanced, flashes of gunfire and the thunder of muskets boomed from out of the trees. Washington's men returned fire. Suddenly, Washington realized they were firing at, and being fired upon, by the other Virginians! He galloped forward between the two lines, furiously knocking guns into the air with his sword. Before anyone else realized what was happening, 14 men were killed and 26 wounded. Unbelievably, once again, no bullet touched Washington though he'd ridden right into the line of fire.

As they continued toward Fort Duquesne Forbes granted Washington the temporary rank of brigadier general and command of the advance troops. Urgently, Washington pressed on. As they crept through the forest, Braddock's fate preyed on everyone's mind. Indians appeared with stories of a thick smoke blanketing the Ohio River Valley.

On November 25, 1758, Washington rode among the smoldering ruins of Fort Duquesne. The French had vanished, burning the fort behind them. This place had haunted and obsessed Washington for four years. Now it was gone without a shot fired. Washington felt he'd made a fool of himself, seeing disasters around every corner and writing to others about his problems with Forbes.

Once again, Washington decided to resign. He'd served Virginia as a soldier for five years. He wrote a letter to his officers thanking them for their service. "If I have acquired any reputation it is from you I derive it. I thank you also for the love and regard you have all along shewn me. It is in this I am rewarded." His officers begged Washington to reconsider. But in January 1759 he returned to civilian life, believing himself finished with the British military forever.

A Friend Describes George Washington

In 1760 George Mercer, an officer, wrote this description of George Washington:

He may be described as being straight as an Indian, measuring 6 feet 2 inches in his stockings, and weighing 175 lbs. . . . His frame is padded with well-developed muscles, indicating great strength. His bones and joints are large as are his hands and feet. He is wide shouldered . . . and has rather long legs and arms. His head is well shaped, though not large. . . . A large and straight rather than a prominent nose; blue-grey penetrating eyes. . . . His face is long rather than broad, with high round cheek bones, and terminates in a good firm chin. He has a clear tho rather colorless pale skin which burns with the sun . . . his mouth is large and generally firmly closed, but which from time to time discloses some defective teeth. . . . His demeanor at all times composed and dignified. His movements and gestures are gracefull, his walk majestic, and he is a splendid horseman.

3

A Virginia Gentleman

efore George Washington left for the Forbes campaign he jumped on his horse and went courting. In March 1758 he called on Martha Dandridge Custis, a wealthy widow. George towered over the brown-haired Widow Custis. She stood barely five feet tall and dressed plainly, but in the best fabrics. People remarked on her beautiful teeth and bright hazel eyes. The Widow Custis had an added beauty—she'd inherited one-third of her husband's vast estate. Her share of the inheritance would become her new husband's property if she remarried.

Martha's gentleness and easy manners charmed George. She offered what

Martha Dandridge Custis.

he needed: the promise of peace, partnership, good sense, and a happy home. Martha had given birth to four children, but two had died. George met Martha's two-year-old daughter, Martha Parke Custis (called Patsy), and four-year-old son, John Parke Custis (called Jacky).

George soon visited Martha again, but the Forbes campaign against Fort Duquesne forced them apart. At some point, the couple decided to wed. Meanwhile, George was writing to Sally Fairfax. For years Sally had flirted, forbidden George to write to her, then written to *him* when he left her alone. For George, loving Sally wasn't happy or peaceful. Less than four months before his marriage to Martha, George wrote to Sally, "The World has no business to know the object of my Love, declared in this manner to—you, when I want to conceal it."

George had already planned to remodel Mount Vernon. As his marriage loomed closer, enlarging his home became even more important. He'd pored over English books on building and design. He added a full second story and a half story, a grand staircase, and some elegant details, such as a marble chimney-piece. The house had a large, open hallway, with the staircase at one end and two rooms on each side: a bedroom, a dining room, a fancy parlor, and another bedroom that later became a second parlor. Upstairs he added four bedrooms.

George married Martha Custis on January 6, 1759. Mary Washington welcomed George's leaving the military and settling down. She wrote to her brother there had been "no end to my trouble while George was in the army, but he has now given it up."

Political Beginnings

The new family traveled to Williamsburg, where George served in the House of Burgesses. Voters around Winchester, where he served as commander of the Virginia army, first elected Washington to the position in 1758. He had lost elections in 1755 and 1757. He later served from his home, Fairfax County. At this time only white men who owned property could vote. Before an election Washington wooed voters with mugs of rum, beer, and cider. After a victory, he often held a celebratory ball for the county.

Between 1758 and 1774 Washington served seven times in the House of Burgesses. The family traveled 160 miles from Mount Vernon to Williamsburg for spring and fall sessions of the assembly. Modest George spoke as little as possible, but listened carefully. One man claimed Washington appeared too bashful to speak. Thomas Jefferson noted his fellow Virginian rarely spoke more than "10 minutes at a time, nor to any but the main point which was to decide the question."

As the 1759 legislative session closed Washington hurried instructions to Mount Ver-

George Washington marries Martha Custis, a wealthy widow with two small children.

Library of Congress, LC-USZ62-68031

non. Construction had not finished and most of the rooms stood empty. But he ordered the house scrubbed, polished, and aired from top to bottom. He also ordered food for the pantry and had the bedsteads set up.

A few months later Washington wrote: "I am now, I believe, fixed at this seat with an agreeable consort [wife] for life, and hope to find more happiness in retirement than I ever experienced amidst a wide and bustling world." The Seven Years' War still raged in North America, but 27-year-old Washington had left all that behind him.

A Gentleman Farmer

After Anne Washington died in 1761, Mount Vernon officially belonged to George. He threw himself into his new life, working harder than most wealthy planters. In purchases large and small, Washington bought more acres surrounding Mount Vernon. Eventually he owned 8,000 acres divided into four working farms, plus the "Mansion House" farm where Mount Vernon stood.

Washington rose before daylight to supervise his ever-expanding farms. As he rode

Mrs. Washington's Duties

"Housewifery" duties for an 18th-century well-to-do woman like Martha Washington meant running her husband's home smoothly and efficiently, with an eye on economy. A woman of Martha's status trained and supervised a small army of enslaved workers. With a basketful of keys to unlock the cupboards and buildings of Mount Vernon, Martha oversaw the cooking, washing, ironing, cleaning, weaving, and sewing for the estate. The healthcare and behavior of the house servants also fell to Martha. She probably kept a medicine chest to treat both family and slaves.

Like other colonial women, Martha raised her children and sewed for her family. She made sure Mount Vernon was kept well supplied with food and drink, including her famous smoked hams. Gracious and graceful as a hostess, she entertained thousands of visitors at her home over the years. People felt drawn to her easy charm and good humor. Abigail Adams would later write, "Mrs. Washington is one of those unassuming characters who create love and esteem."

around, a pack of hound dogs bred for fox hunting surged after his horse. At one time Washington's male dogs included Tartar, Jupiter, Trueman, Drunkard, Vulcan, and Rover, while the females included Truelove, June, Duchess, Lady, and Sweetlips!

Washington studied farming books from England. He liked the challenge of figuring out problems, experimenting, and tinkering. Mount

Washington oversees his farms while Jacky and Patsy play.

Library of Congress, LC-USZ62-3912

Vernon, he discovered, had poor soil, not suited for growing Virginia's cash crop, tobacco. Washington mixed different soils and fertilizers and tested how fast wheat, oats, and barley grew in each. His diaries filled with notes about farming and weather. He tried new crops, like Virginia grapes for wine, and bought the newest farm machines from England.

George and Martha ordered lavishly from England, and their debt rose. He often penned angry letters to his agent in London, Robert Cary. Why did he bother sending measurements for clothes, when the garments arrived and did not fit? Why did farm tools and machinery arrive missing pieces so they wouldn't work? One time, George and six-year-old Patsy searched the ship for a missing doll they'd ordered. The doll had not been packed and would not arrive at Mount Vernon for another year.

In 1768 Washington sent detailed instructions for a new carriage "in the newest taste . . . to be made of the best seasoned wood, and by a celebrated workman." The agent's invoice promised "a handsome chariot made of the best materials, handsomely carved." But within two months the Washingtons' expensive carriage fell apart; the cheap, unseasoned wood split in long cracks.

It didn't help that Washington generously loaned money he didn't always have. He supported some of his nephews and nieces. He helped friends and those in need, including soldiers he'd known in the French and Indian War. He felt obliged to help those who asked. Dying neighbors begged Washington to manage their estates and serve as guardian to their children. He helped pay for the education of friends' children. If Washington could not help someone, he felt bad, and wrote detailed letters explaining why.

Sew a Lady's Cap

Women usually wore a cap both indoors and out in public. A cap displayed her modesty. It also covered her hair, which was seldom washed, for people believed bathing was bad for their health. Caps also kept a woman's hair out of the way while she cooked and did chores.

Materials

String
Pencil
Ruler
Scissors
2 sheets of poster board
1 yard white muslin, cotton, or linen fabric
White thread
Large-eyed sewing needle
60 inches lace trim
60 inches colored satin ribbon, $\frac{1}{8}$ inch wide

Tie the string to the pencil. Cut the string to measure 9 inches. Hold the loose end of the string in the center of one of the sheets of poster board. Pull the pencil until the string is tight and draw a circle around the board. The circle should measure 18 inches across (the diameter). Repeat on the second sheet of poster board *but cut the string to measure 7½ inches this time.* This new circle should measure 15 inches across. Cut out both circles. These are your patterns.

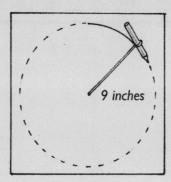

9 inches

Place the larger pattern on the fabric and cut out a circle of material the same size. With the white thread, sew the lace trim around the edge of the fabric circle. Center the smaller pattern on top of the fabric and lightly trace the pattern onto it.

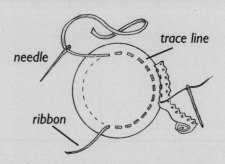

needle
trace line
ribbon

Thread the satin ribbon through the needle and push it into the fabric along the traced circle. Don't pull it all the way through—leave about 8 inches hanging out. Now sew the ribbon around the traced circle, going up and down through the cloth every 1–1½ inches. At the end, leave another 8 inches hanging free. Gather the cap by bunching it along the ribbon to fit your head. Tie the ribbon ends into a bow at the front of the cap.

The Ham That Got Away

Washington enjoyed telling the story of Vulcan's dash through the house while the family sat at dinner. The dog timed his leap, whisked a ham off the table, then pounded outdoors. After a chase, the ham was rescued, but they couldn't eat it. The canine theft of one of her prized hams did not amuse Martha, but George thought the escapade funny.

But his debt embarrassed Washington. Like other Virginia gentlemen, he felt pressured to live up to his rank in society. A man dreaded his neighbors gossiping at the next dance about his decaying fortunes. But expenses had "swallowed up before I knew where I was all the money I got by marriage." He vowed to make Mount Vernon run more smoothly.

The Washingtons entertain guests outdoors at Mount Vernon.
Library of Congress, LC-USZ62-77268

After five years as a tobacco planter, Washington gave up. The plant ruined the soil while needing too many workers and too much care. "Every villainous worm that has had an existence since the days of Noah" attacked his tobacco, he wrote to his brother-in-law. "How unkind it was of Noah . . . to suffer such a brood of vermin to get a berth in the ark."

A planter and his only crop lay at the mercy of weather as well as worms. After that he lay at the mercy of his London agent. "Certain I am no person in Virginia takes more pains to make their tobacco fine than I do," he complained to Robert Cary, "and 'tis hard that I should not be as well rewarded for it."

Washington decided to switch from a tobacco crop to grains such as corn and wheat. He'd save money growing the huge amounts of grain needed at Mount Vernon to feed people and farm animals. He also sold his grain to local merchants, who paid him cash. By 1766 Washington did not grow a single tobacco leaf. Instead, he harvested 7,000 bushels of wheat and 10,000 bushels of corn, and each year his crop increased. Enslaved workers who had once labored in tobacco fields switched to jobs like weaving. By 1770 Washington had branched out even more, building a mill to grind his grain–and his neighbors' grain for a price. He also started a fishery and sold thousands of pounds of salted fish.

Washington also enjoyed planning Mount Vernon's gardens. He plotted flower beds, vegetable gardens, herb gardens, and fruit orchards, and had one garden just for experimenting with different plants to test what would grow in Virginia's climate. He designed paths that wandered through decorative hedges and even created a "wilderness" area.

Washington struggled to make his farms more self-sufficient. Washington sent extra money to England, paying down his British debts. He decided to buy more goods from colonial merchants, men he could deal with more easily than British agents if he had a problem. As a young man he'd pursued a commission in the British army with fiery ambition. Now Great Britain edged further away from the center of George Washington's world.

A Busy Life

The Washingtons enjoyed a busy social life, visiting neighbors and welcoming friends, relatives, and passing strangers to Mount Vernon. Between 1768 and 1775 George and Martha entertained nearly 2,000 guests! Both Washingtons loved a house full of company, but sometimes the family needed privacy, too. In 1774 George began enlarging Mount Vernon again. He added a private wing for the family on one side of the main house that included a private study for himself and upstairs a master bedroom that also served as Martha's office. On the other side of the house he planned a large two-story-tall room for entertaining. He also

Slavery at Mount Vernon

Washington hired white indentured workers and master craftsmen such as builders and gardeners. But enslaved people performed most of the labor on Washington's plantations. Slaves served as blacksmiths, barrel makers, carpenters, shoemakers, weavers, and laundresses. Others mended fences and dug drainage ditches. Most slaves worked in the fields. Enslaved house "servants" at Mount Vernon included the cook and kitchen help, a waiter, a butler, a seamstress, and personal servants for George, Martha, and the children.

Some of Washington's slaves fled to freedom. Washington had no sympathy for a slave that ran away, and he advertised for runaway slaves in Virginia newspapers. Washington made one slave, named Tom, an overseer. But later Washington labeled Tom "both a rogue and a runaway." Washington put Tom on a ship sailing to the Caribbean and instructed the ship's captain to sell him.

In the years before the American Revolution Washington did not question the slave system of his society. A slave was his property. When a slave died, he noted the cash value he'd lost. Washington believed he had a moral duty to not treat his slaves harshly. Generally, Washington did not break up slave families by selling members away.

By 1765 Washington owned 78 slaves; he also kept slaves that belonged to the Custis estate. Slave births greatly outnumbered deaths on his plantations. When he rode off to the Revolutionary War in 1775, he owned 135 enslaved people.

Plant a Garden

Washington ordered seeds and flower bulbs from Europe. His pleasure gardens included dozens of plants: parrot tulips, Crown Imperial lilies, hollyhocks, peonies, primroses, heliotropes, larkspurs, figs, flowering cherry trees, poppies, and boxwood hedges.

He planted trees and shrubs and designed decorative garden beds. The kitchen garden supplied vegetables, fruits, and herbs for cooking. It had asparagus, beets, beans, spinach, peas, herbs, fruit trees (apple and pear), artichokes, onions, lettuce, raspberries, and strawberries. Washington also harvested pecan and hickory nuts from trees he had planted.

Materials

Sunny garden spot or a plant container, such as a plastic or clay pot (be sure it has a drain hole in the bottom)

If you plant in a container: some gravel, packing peanuts, or a broken clay pot for drainage

If you plant in a container: bag of potting soil

If you plant in a garden: manure

Selection of herbs, flowers, or vegetables already started in a container, or a packet of seeds

Watering can, or bucket and cup

If you use a plant container:

Place a bit of gravel, packing peanuts, or pieces of a broken clay pot at the bottom of the container. If you are using plants that have already started growing, add some potting soil. Take the plants out of their store container and set them into the pot. Use your fingers to loosen the roots a bit if they are tightly packed. Add more potting soil around the plants, filling the container to about 1 inch below the rim, and pat it down firmly. Water the plants until water runs out the bottom. Set your plants in a sunny spot and keep them watered. You may have to water them every day if the weather is hot.

If you use seeds:

Read the directions on the seed packet. Fill the container with potting soil, poke the seeds into it, and pat firm some more soil on the top. Don't plant them too deeply. Gently water the seeds each day. When the baby plants are a few inches tall you can thin them out by pulling out some of the sprouts so the rest will have room to grow. Keep watering!

If you use a sunny garden spot in the yard:

Prepare the soil by digging into it and mixing in manure as fertilizer. Be sure the soil is smooth and raked without chunks of dirt when you are finished. If you are using plants that have already started growing, dig a hole big enough for the plant. Take the plants out of the store container. Loosen the roots if they are wound tightly. Slip the plant into the hole and fill the hole with water. Push dirt over the hole and pat it down firmly around the plant. If you are using seeds, read the packet directions. You will plant the seeds directly into the soil and water them gently. Thin the baby seedlings by pulling some out so the rest have room to grow. Keep watering!

added an original touch for the times. A long porch, or piazza, stretched across the back of the house. Here guests could sit on bottle-green chairs and watch the Potomac flow by.

In 1768 Washington attended church 15 times, but went fox hunting on 49 occasions. That year he also attended two balls, three plays, a puppet show, and one horse race. Washington still loved to dance–especially to lively tunes. A gambler at heart, Washington bet on cockfights and card games. He spent freely on raffle tickets, attempting to win a necklace, an encyclopedia, a carriage, and land. Washington smoked the long-stemmed clay pipes so popular in Virginia, which he bought by the case. When away on business, he stayed with friends or rented a room.

Like any gentleman, Washington collected books. His personal library contained over 880 titles on farming, history, geography, law, military strategy, and literature. He also owned a number of pamphlets and maps. Washington believed books helped educate a man, but education needed a practical slant, too, like his own training as a surveyor. He also believed most people learned best through "dear bought experience."

Washington did not know Greek or Latin like other founding fathers. He did know works of Shakespeare. His favorite play, though, was Joseph Addison's *Cato* (1713), the story of a noble Roman soldier who kills himself to save his country. Washington also

George and Martha's bedroom at Mount Vernon.

Courtesy of the Mount Vernon Ladies' Association

A Belief in Providence

Like most Virginians, George belonged to the Anglican Church, the official church of England. He first became a church "vestryman" in 1762. A person in this elected position helped run the nonreligious side of church business. But Washington was rather ho-hum about established churches. He believed in God, a force he often called Providence, as a higher power that ruled events. This was a power he felt human beings could never understand or know. Washington felt "that the road to heaven" should be the one a person found "most direct, plainest, easiest." People were free to choose that road themselves.

Washington returns from a fox hunt.
Library of Congress, LC-USZ62-121764

favored Roman writer Seneca's works about man's search for perfection.

One way Washington unleashed his aggressive, gambler side was in land speculation. He loved to seek out and buy land, especially western lands. His knowledge of surveying and maps served Washington well. He also knew how to use his political influence to get the lands he wanted.

Back in 1754, Lieutenant Governor Dinwiddie promised land bounties to Virginia's French and Indian War soldiers. But nothing came of this promise. When the Seven Years' War ended in 1763, Great Britain issued a proclamation forbidding colonists from moving west over the Allegheny Mountains. Britain hoped to prevent clashes between Native Americans and the white colonists.

Washington, however, never saw the proclamation "in any other light . . . than as a temporary expedient to quiet the minds of the Indians. . . . It must fall, of course, in a few years." Washington pushed the Virginia government for the lands promised to war veterans. In 1769 Governor Botetcourt agreed to a survey of western lands. Washington took on the job. He used Virginia newspapers to alert war veterans to the land bounties. He also asked his brother Charles to secretly see if any veterans would be willing to sell Charles their land bounty rights.

In October 1770 Washington set off on a nine-week trip with Dr. James Craik and fellow surveyor William Crawford. They canoed down the Ohio River to the Great Kanawha River. Washington drew rough surveys and cut trees to mark boundaries for land lots. When the time came to distribute the lots, about 30 percent were registered in Washington's name, including some of the best parcels. A few people later complained about Washington's dealings. This upset Washington, who felt he'd taken on the risk and expense, and if not for him, "not a single acre of land would ever have been obtained." Washington, the land speculator, eventually owned over 60,000 acres, including the land where Fort Necessity once stood.

Play a Game of Whist

One of George Washington's favorite card games was whist, a popular game during the 18th and 19th centuries. In many ways, whist is similar to the modern card game of bridge.

Materials

4 people
Deck of 52 playing cards

Partners face each other across the card table. People play their cards going clockwise. One person shuffles the deck and deals each player 13 cards. The highest card is the Ace, followed by King, Queen, Jack, 10, 9, 8, 7, 6, 5, 4, 3, and 2, which is the lowest card. The final card dealt to the dealer starts the game. It is turned up and laid on the table so everyone can see what suit (spade, heart, diamond, or club) it is. This is the "trump" suit—the Ace of trump is the highest card in the deck. Any trump card is higher than a card of any other suit.

The player on the dealer's left lays a card on the table. The other players in turn must "follow suit" by playing a card from the same suit if they have any. If a player does not have a card to follow suit, he or she can put any card down, including a card from the trump suit. The round, or "trick," is taken by the person with the highest card in the suit, or if someone played a trump card, by the highest trump. Whoever won the trick leads the next card.

Play all 13 tricks. Make neat stacks of the cards you win in each trick so you can count how many tricks your side has taken. The partners with the most tricks at the end of the hand score 1 point for each trick over 6. The next person deals and another hand is played. The first team to reach 5 points wins the game.

The First Portrait

George Washington became one of the most painted and sculpted men in history. It all started in 1772 when Washington sat for a portrait painted by artist Charles Wilson Peale. George dug out his old uniform for the occasion. But he felt silly posing for the artist:

I am now under the hands of Mr. Peale, but in so grave, so sullen a mood, and now and then under the influence of Morpheus [sleepy] when some critical strokes are making, that I fancy the skill of this gentleman's pencil will be put to it in describing to the world the manner of man I am.

Stepfather and Stepchildren

Piece by piece, Washington built a great estate, one he must have hoped to pass on to a child of his own. But at some point George and Martha realized they would not have children of their own. This must have been a great disappointment, but George still had Martha's two children to help raise.

Washington felt a stepfather should be "generous and attentive." Carefully, George tracked every penny spent on Jacky and Patsy's clothes, toys, and education. He didn't want anyone to think he took advantage of their Custis fortune.

George and Martha both spoiled the children. Every year he ordered chests of toys and schoolbooks from England for the little ones. Both children dressed in London finery befitting their station in life. Four-year-old Jacky had silver shoe and knee buckles. At age seven he wore a silver lace-trimmed hat. Patsy donned a silk coat when she was only six. Each child had his or her own enslaved servant. Jacky's servant, Little Julius, was only four years older than the Custis boy.

When Jacky was seven, Washington hired the lad's first tutor. But Jacky proved a lazy student. With Martha's permission, George sent the boy to a private academy in Maryland. He advised the schoolmaster to watch over Jacky, "as he is a promising boy, the last of his family, and will possess a very large fortune." Washington also hoped the school would make young Custis "fit for more useful purposes than a horse racer." But all his life Jacky preferred horse racing, dogs, hunting, and merrymaking to his studies. After all, Jacky knew he'd become master of a very wealthy estate, so why work too hard? Washington believed the more wealth and power a man held, "the more pains should be taken to enlarge his mind." He cared for Jacky, but often felt frustrated with the boy he had helped raise since a toddler.

George enrolled Jacky at King's College (now Columbia) in New York. While there, young Custis became secretly engaged to Eleanor Calvert of Maryland. Washington counseled postponing the wedding until Jacky grew older and finished his education. Jacky wed anyway at age 19.

Patsy Custis learned lessons at home and also practiced dancing and music. But when she was 12 Patsy suffered a seizure, the first sign she had epilepsy. Martha hovered and worried over her daughter's health. The Washingtons tried everything 18th-century medicine offered to help Patsy. She swallowed musk pills and purges, and was bled by her physicians. She wore an iron ring. Vials of medicines arrived from caring friends. The family visited Warm Springs, hoping for a cure. One doctor ordered more exercise and forbade certain foods; Patsy's body should be kept cool and each day she should drink barley water. But nothing helped.

On June 19, 1773, when she was 17, Patsy rose from the dinner table at about 4:00 P.M. Soon after, she suffered a seizure. In less than two minutes she lay dead "without uttering a word, a groan, or scarce a sigh," George wrote to Martha's sister and brother-in-law. He could not describe "the distress of this family . . . when I inform you that yesterday removed the sweet innocent girl."

Jacky and George, through Martha, shared equally in the money left to Patsy by her father. George used his share to help pay off his debt to Cary & Company, his London agents.

The Road Toward Revolution

With the end of the Seven Years' War, Great Britain staggered beneath its own burden of debt. The British government needed to raise money, and Parliament decided the American colonies must pay their share. Up until now only the legislatures elected in each colony had the power to tax the colonists. But Parliament passed a series of taxes in Great Britain for the colonists to pay.

Colonists complained they had no representation in the Parliament—it was unfair to pass taxes they had no voice in. But many members of Parliament believed if they did not

A 19th-century print based on Peale's portrait of Washington at age 40.

Design a Bookplate

In 1772 Washington ordered an engraved bookplate bearing the Washington coat of arms, to label the inside cover of his books. (Washington often signed his books on the title page, as well.) His bookplate carried the Latin motto *Exitus Acta Probat* from the coat of arms: "The result justifies the deed."

Materials

Ruler

Heavy weight paper

Colored pens and markers

Scissors

Photocopy machine (optional)

Glue stick

Using the ruler, draw a 4-inch-by-3-inch rectangle onto the heavy weight paper. Design your bookplate. It must have a place to show the name of the book owner, but you can make it as fancy as you wish. Try creating a border using patterns of scrolls, leaves, geometric designs, stars, or whatever you choose. You can also include a favorite phrase or motto as Washington did. Or your bookplate can be as simple as "This Book Belongs to _____." You can take your bookplate and have photocopies made if you wish. Cut out your bookplate. Center it inside the cover of a book you own and glue it down.

---

have taxation power over America "then America is at once a kingdom of itself."

Like many colonists Washington had his complaints against Great Britain. Sitting in the House of Burgesses he watched the unfolding crisis between Great Britain and her colonies firsthand. When Americans protested the Stamp Act taxes of 1765 and boycotted British goods to underscore their point, Washington took a practical view: "Many luxuries which we lavish our substance to Great Britain for, can well be dispensed with, while the necessities of life are (mostly) to be made within ourselves."

In response to new taxes, the Townshend Acts of 1767, Washington helped George Mason, a friend and neighbor, write a list of goods Virginians should not buy from England. Washington, however, did not leap wholeheartedly into the anti-British movement swelling in the colonies. He preferred "balancing [events] in my mind and giving the subject the fairest consideration." He believed, and hoped, the problems with Great Britain would shake themselves out. He wasn't sure the vio-

This British cartoon from 1766 shows a funeral for the Stamp Act, repealed after American protests and boycotts.

The Intolerable Acts proved a turning point for Washington. With his fellow Burgesses, Washington offered his support to Massachusetts, a move that angered Virginia's royal governor, who dissolved the legislature on the spot. Washington wrote to George William Fairfax that Great Britain "may rely on it that Americans will never be tax'd without their own consent that the cause of Boston . . . ever will be considered as the cause of America." But like most colonists, Washington wanted his rights as an English citizen upheld. The notion of independence from Great Britain was not yet in the air.

With George Mason, Washington drafted the Fairfax Resolves at Mount Vernon. The Resolves, adopted at a July 1774 meeting of Fairfax County officials, pledged support for Massachusetts and renewed the call to stop importing goods from Britain. People worried that British punishments forced on Massachusetts could happen in their colony, as well. It seemed a good idea to prepare for the worst. Militia companies throughout Virginia sought Washington's advice on training and military matters.

An unofficial meeting "to deliberate and consult" called as many Burgesses as possible back to Williamsburg in August. The gathered

lent reaction in many towns—mobs beating crown officials and tarring and feathering tax collectors—provided any solutions. Washington needed proof Britain had "a regular plan at the expense of law and justice to overthrow our constitutional rights and liberties."

When news of the December 1773 Boston Tea Party reached Virginia, Washington feared the destruction of the British tea would carry harsh penalties for the colonies. King George III and Parliament *were* furious. The Coercive Acts, labeled the Intolerable Acts in the colonies, punished Massachusetts. The crown closed Boston Harbor to all trade and amassed troops to control the town.

Washington served in the First Continental Congress in Carpenter's Hall, Philadelphia, September 1774.

A Virginia Loyalist, or supporter of Great Britain, is forced to sign a document by a Williamsburg mob. Tar and feathers wait nearby in this February 1775 British cartoon.

members elected Washington as one of seven Virginia delegates to the First Continental Congress, a meeting of the colonies in Philadelphia.

Washington's beliefs had shifted. He wrote to his friend Bryan Fairfax, "The Acts of a British Parliament are no longer Govern'd by the Principles of justice–that it is trampling upon the Valuable Rights of American's, confirmed to them by Charter, & the Constitution [the British] themselves boast of." And after ignoring appeals and petitions from the colonies, George now felt Britain clearly showed "a fixed and uniform plan to tax us."

In Philadelphia Washington met leaders from other colonies. In meetings, but also over dinner and at tavern tables, they debated how to deal with their tense situation. Washington's tall figure and military bearing impressed other delegates. The Congress decided to send King George III a Declaration of Colonial Rights and Grievances. They also passed the Continental Association, a nonimportation agreement. This mass colonial boycott aimed to force change by hitting Britain's pocketbook. Congress agreed to meet again in May 1775 if the situation failed to improve.

By the following year events had decayed further. Virginia again sent Washington as a delegate to the Second Continental Congress. News that Massachusetts's militias had fought British soldiers at Lexington and Concord (April 19) darkened the minds of the delegates.

Most felt deeply shocked that the king's troops had spilled the blood of His Majesty's own subjects. Militias from around New England, about 9,000 men, now surrounded British troops in Boston.

"The Command I Am Honored With"

Washington assumed he'd return from Congress, and if bloodshed continued, take command of Virginia regiments. He decided to wear his old uniform to the Continental Congress. Did he mean to show that Virginia was prepared to fight, or that he himself was ready to do his duty once again?

Washington served on all committees dealing with military matters. Most delegates hoped for restored harmony between Great Britain and the colonies. They blamed Parliament and would ask King George III to grant his colonies relief. Many believed the colonists must fight only to defend themselves.

On June 14, 1775, Congress voted to raise six companies of soldiers from Pennsylvania, Maryland, and Virginia to join those in Massachusetts. Congress, not the individual colonies, would pay the soldiers. This Continental Army, "for the defense of American liberty," urgently needed a commander.

Washington's modesty kept him from pushing for the job. He may not have even wanted it. Yes, he had military experience, but Washington knew he'd made mistakes in his military past. But he was older and wiser now.

The Congress's vote was unanimous. They elected 43-year-old Washington commander in chief, shoving him into the spotlight of oncoming war. On June 16 Washington accepted "supreme command" of the Continental Army. But instead of inspiring the delegates with bold words promising victories, he quietly confessed, "I do not think myself equal to the command I am honored with." He asked Congress to pay his expenses, but turned down a salary.

Washington knew that Great Britain could hit the colonies with thousands of well-trained, well-supplied men, and that the Royal Navy ruled the seas. The colonies had no navy. So far, the Continental Army had one official soldier–George Washington.

George would ride straight to Massachusetts. On June 18 he sat down to write to Martha. He offered practical advice on money matters and told her he'd written out a will:

You may believe me, my dear Patsy [Martha's nickname], when I assure you . . . that, so far from seeking this appointment, I have used every

John Adams of Massachusetts nominates Washington for commander in chief of the Continental Army.

Library of Congress, LC-USZ62-55279

endeavor in my power to avoid it, not only from my unwillingness to part with you and the family, but from a consciousness of its being a trust too great for my capacity. . . . I shall rely, therefore, confidently on that Providence, which has heretofore preserved and been bountiful to me, not doubting but that I shall return safe to you in the fall. I shall feel no pain from the toil of the danger of the campaign; my unhappiness will flow from the uneasiness I know you will feel from being left alone.

To his brother, John, Washington confided, "I am Imbarked on a wide Ocean, . . . from whence, perhaps, no safe harbour is to be found."

Washington wrote to Martha that he'd return home in the fall, a few months away. As it turned out, George enjoyed only one brief visit to Mount Vernon in the next eight years.

Washington crossing the Delaware.

Courtesy of the Mount Vernon Ladies' Association

4

"The Momentous Duty"

n July 3, 1775, the new commander in chief met his army of New England militiamen at Cambridge, Massachusetts. Chaos reigned. Soldiers ignored orders. Privies (outhouses) had not been dug. Washington immediately began organizing, planning, and strengthening American defenses. He forbade swearing and drunkenness. He demanded "exact discipline," the "life and soul of an army." Failed discipline brought only "Hazard, Disorder and Confusion."

William Emerson, a chaplain for Washington's troops, noted the changes. "Great distinction is made between officers and soldiers. Everyone is made to know his place and keep it, or be tied

The General's Headquarters

Washington and his staff usually rented a private citizen's home for their crowded headquarters. Here they slept, ate, entertained, planned strategies, and carried on other war business. On campaigns during the summer and fall, Washington's tent served as his headquarters, with a portable writing desk and a folding cot for sleeping.

up and receive thirty or forty lashes according to his crime. Thousands are at work from four till eleven o'clock in the morning. It is surprising how much work has been done."

Washington discovered that the army had only 36 precious barrels of gunpowder, fewer than nine rounds of ammunition per soldier. If the British attacked, the Americans could never defend themselves. Washington hid this discouraging news from everyone but a few key advisors.

His days overflowed with work and worry. He barely slept. He worried about home. Should Martha move from Mount Vernon? Would people who owed him money pay up so he could repay his own debts? He wasn't sure he even trusted the New Englanders. "Generally speaking," he confided to a cousin, "[they are] the most indifferent Kind of people I ever saw . . . an exceedingly dirty and nasty people."

The New England soldiers and officers felt the same mistrust toward the Virginian forced on them by the Congress. But Washington won them over. He carried himself with dignity and charmed people he met. The soldiers knew they needed discipline to succeed. They also respected Washington's thriftiness. He refused a salary for his service. He made the best out of very little. And he worked hard, never leaving camp except for meetings with government officials.

"I pity our poor General, who has a greater burden on his shoulders and more difficulties to struggle with than I think should fall to the share of so good a man," wrote James Warren, president of the Massachusetts Congress. "I see he is fatigued and worried."

Boston

When Washington arrived, New England militias had British troops pinned inside Boston. After the British took heavy losses at the Battle of Bunker Hill on June 17, 1775, British generals realized they could only replace their soldiers with men brought all the way from Europe. So for the moment, both sides sat and waited.

As the weeks went on and autumn approached, Washington worried how he'd supply his army over the winter. He wished "Congress to bestow a little more attention to the Affairs of this army, which suffers exceedingly." He had no money and little gunpowder or weapons, and "when we shall be called upon to take the Field, shall not have a Tent to lay in." he wrote. He proposed attacking the British in Boston, but his generals convinced him an attack would fail.

Worse yet, how much of his army would vanish at the end of December when the soldiers' enlistments ended? Washington believed the system of short-term enlistment put the

Make Washington's Commander in Chief Flag

Materials

Paper

Pencil

Ruler

Scissors

Piece of white fabric

Piece of solid dark blue fabric, 2 feet by 3
    feet

½-inch dowel rod

Stapler

Fabric glue

Draw and cut out a paper pattern for a
single star. The star should be about 5 inches
across. Washington's flag had stars with six
points. Using the paper pattern as a guide,
cut 13 stars out of the white fabric.

Spread out the blue fabric. Fold over
1 to 2 inches of fabric along one of the
short sides. Staple it down all along the edge
to form a pocket for the dowel rod, and
slide the rod through. Lay the stars out on
the blue field as shown. Use fabric glue to
attach the stars to the blue field.

With permission and adult help, tap two
nails into the wall and rest the dowel rod
on them to hang your flag.

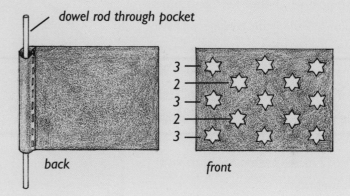

dowel rod through pocket

back

front

3
2
3
2
3

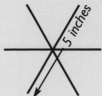

5 inches

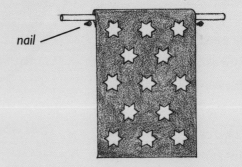

nail

A Poem for a General

In October 1775 Phillis Wheatley, a former slave, sent Washington a letter and poem. To honor her "great poetical Genius," Washington considered having the poem published. But he decided not to. Since the poem praised him, he didn't want to seem vain. "I thank you most sincerely for your polite notice of me in the elegant lines enclosed," he wrote back to her in February 1776. He invited Phillis to visit him at Cambridge.

Phillis Wheatley had been born in Africa, captured, and sold into slavery when she was about seven years old. The family that owned Phillis taught her to read and write and eventually freed her. Wheatley started writing poetry as a child and became the first African American to publish a book. She died in 1784 and one of her last poems, "Liberty and Peace," celebrated the end of the American Revolution.

Phillis Wheatley.
Library of Congress, LC-USZ62-12533

Americans at a great disadvantage against professional British soldiers. Just when he'd spent months drilling raw recruits into soldiers prepared for battle, they would go home!

Months passed outside Boston. Washington hated waiting for the British to make a move. Finally, in early March, under cover of darkness, he ordered Dorchester Heights above Boston fortified with cannon. British general William Howe awoke to find American artillery leveled on his army. He decided to abandon Boston. A whirlwind few weeks later, British ships crammed with officials, soldiers, and thousands of fleeing Loyalists (colonial supporters of Great Britain) sailed out of the city.

In a letter to his brother John, George Washington briefly allowed himself a pat on the back:

I have been here months . . . with what will scarcely be believed. . . . Not thirty rounds of musket cartridges a man. . . . We have maintained our ground against the enemy, . . . and we have disbanded one army and recruited another within musket shot of two and twenty regiments, the [best] of the British army, and at last have beat them.

Hard Times in New York

Washington believed the British fleet would next land in New York, a town of over 20,000 people, but still an area of farmland and forest.

Soldiers in New York crowd around Washington to hear the Declaration of Independence in this 1870 woodcut from Harper's Weekly.

Library of Congress, LC-USZ62-96106

He marched the Continental Army south, reaching New York in mid-April 1776. He had too few men to occupy the areas of Brooklyn Heights, Harlem Heights, Long Island, Man-hattan Island, and Staten Island, and protect the Hudson and East Rivers.

On July 9, a few days after the first British forces landed on Staten Island, Washington gathered the army and read an incredible document to the troops. Only days before in Philadelphia, Congress had approved a Declaration of Independence, cutting the ties between Great Britain and the free and independent states of America. This war, these soldiers, would fight for the birth of a new nation.

But Washington knew each man viewed his own state or region as his country. Could he blend men from different areas into a single unit? "The Honor and Success of the army, and the safety of our bleeding Country, depends upon harmony and good agreement with each other," he urged. "Let all distinctions of Nations, Countries, and Provinces therefore be lost."

By August, 32,000 British soldiers camped on Staten Island. The masts of their vast fleet appeared like a forest on the water. Washington commanded about 19,000 men.

The Continental Army suffered a series of failures in New York. The British advanced onto Long Island, captured Brooklyn Heights, and opened the East River. During the Battle of Long Island on August 27, American troops broke ranks and ran in total chaos. Washington lost 1,400 men in battle, and thousands of others simply slipped away for home. The Connecticut militia dwindled from 8,000 men to

Washington's "Motley Crew"

British general Howe's secretary Ambrose Serle claimed, on September 2, 1776, that Washington's army "will not fight at any Rate, unless they are sure of a Retreat. Their army is the strangest that ever was collected: Old men of 60, Boys of 14, and Blacks of all ages, and ragged for the most part, compose the motley crew."

2,000. "The dependence Congress has placed upon the militia . . . I fear will totally ruin our Cause," Washington complained to his brother John. The militias were not "worth the bread they eat," Washington exploded to his cousin Lund.

The Americans retreated behind Brooklyn Heights. Hidden by the night, Washington quietly withdrew 9,000 men to Manhattan on August 29. A few weeks later, when the British attacked Manhattan from land and water, American soldiers ran again, dumping their guns and packs. Washington galloped toward the firing, his horse an island in a sea of fleeing men.

He threw his hat to the ground. "Are these the men with whom I am to defend America?" he cried. In fury he lashed at the running men with his riding whip. "Good God! Have I got such troops as these?"

When British troops appeared over the hill, Washington sat unmoving on his horse. Several aides galloped up, grabbed the reins, and pulled his horse away. General Nathanael Greene, who would become one of Washington's best friends, wrote that the commander felt "so vexed at the infamous conduct of his troops that he sought death rather than life." Washington's army regrouped on Harlem Heights. The next day, American troops did not flee. They stood their ground and the British soldiers ran.

Washington dashed letter after letter off to Congress begging for an army with long-term enlistments that "would be daily improving." He wanted militia troops as support only for a main army in which men served at least three years. This was the only way, Washington believed, to create a disciplined fighting force instead of always having raw soldiers. But many in Congress feared a well-trained, long-term army loyal to a strong leader like Washington. History showed that many such men had used their armies to grasp power for themselves.

By the end of October, Washington had evacuated Harlem Heights and moved most of the army to White Plains, New York. He'd left soldiers behind at Fort Washington and Fort Lee to shut the Hudson River to the British. Following a British attack at White Plains, Washington withdrew again, dividing his army to protect New Jersey and Philadelphia. He ordered another force under General Charles Lee to block any British advance toward New England.

Charles Lee, a one-time professional soldier in the British army, fumed that Washington had command of the Continental forces. He bad-mouthed Washington to everyone he could. "Had I the powers," Lee wrote to friends in Congress, "I could do you much good."

Washington rushed back when the British attacked Fort Washington in November. But he could only helplessly watch the capture of nearly 3,000 American soldiers. Washington continued his retreat through New Jersey and crossed the Delaware River into Pennsylvania.

Design a Recruiting Poster

General Washington always needed more soldiers. Every state, every town was supposed to raise troops. What can you say to make young men run to the recruiting officer? What will catch their eye? Many recruiting officers targeted teenage boys who didn't have children, wives, farms, or businesses to leave. This poster promises a bounty of $12 to sign up, "good and handsome cloathing," and a "large and ample ration" of food each day. Were these promises kept?

Materials

Sheet of poster board

Ruler

Pencil

Colored markers

Using a ruler, lightly make lines on the poster board. Write your recruiting advertisement. Put the most important messages in eye-catching big letters. Make the poster dramatic! Make promises!

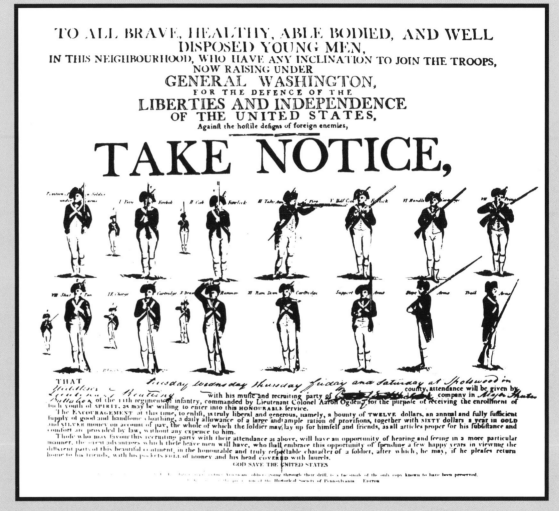

A recruiting broadside.

Library of Congress, LC-USZ62-35262

Washington and the American Revolution, 1775–1783

NEW HAMPSHIRE

Bunker Hill/Breed's Hill
Charlestown

NEW YORK

New York City
Brooklyn Heights

Boston

MASSACHUSETTS

RHODE ISLAND
CONNECTICUT

Newburgh

Morristown
Delaware River
Germantown

West Point
White Plains
Long Island

Staten Island

PENNSYLVANIA

Valley Forge
Brandywine Creek

NEW JERSEY

Monmouth

Princeton
Trenton

Philadelphia

Annapolis
Mount Vernon

MARYLAND

APPALACHIAN MOUNTAINS

DELAWARE

Williamsburg

Chesapeake Bay

VIRGINIA

Proclamation Line of 1763

Yorktown

ATLANTIC OCEAN

NORTH CAROLINA

He wrote to Lee that they must now combine their forces. As the British advanced into Pennsylvania Congress packed their papers and quill pens and fled Philadelphia. "I tremble for Philadelphia," Washington wrote to Lund. "Nothing in my opinion but General Lee's speedy arrival who has been long expected . . . can save it."

Lee dragged his heels. When he finally showed up Washington graciously offered him the chance to shine. Washington would allow Lee to attack the British, if the situation arose, without consulting the commander in chief. Lee galloped to a tavern to celebrate his new chance for glory—and was promptly captured by the British!

A Much-Needed Victory

As 1776 drew to a close, Washington desperately needed even a shadow of a victory, but he wondered how he could attack across the Delaware River. The nearest enemy garrison held roughly 3,000 Hessian troops, German soldiers hired by King George III to fight his rebellious subjects. In the dark hours of Christmas night, 2,400 American soldiers trudged through rain, sleet, and snow to the Delaware River, where horses and men were loaded onto waiting boats. Ice coated the decks. Men and animals fought for balance as hunks of ice struck the vessels. Water sprayed over the sides, freezing on the men's clothes. By four in the morning the entire force had reached the other shore. The army began a nine-mile frozen march through a heavy curtain of snow.

They surprised the Hessians at Trenton. The Americans captured 900 prisoners of war and began the march back, this time dragging seized cannon, guns, and supplies with them. But even in victory, Washington faced losing his army in just a few days. He tried to rally the men:

My brave fellows, you have done all I asked you to do, and more than could be reasonably expected, but your country is at stake: your wives, your houses, and all that you hold dear. You have worn yourselves out with fatigues and hardships, but we know not how to spare you. . . . The present is . . . the crisis which is to decide our destiny.

About half the men stayed. News of the victory brought more recruits to Washington's camp.

Washington's force prepares to cross the Delaware River on Christmas night 1776.
Library of Congress, LC-USZ62-61047

1777

A British army under Lord Charles Cornwallis moved quickly to trap the Americans. Washington left decoy campfires burning through the night while the troops slipped away. A few days later near Princeton, New Jersey, the Americans met two British regiments advancing to aid Cornwallis. Washington galloped ahead to join the advance guard's fight. Once again, he seemed possessed of a charmed life–he rode right between the two lines as they fired. One of Washington's aides covered his face in horror so he wouldn't see the commander in chief killed. But while others fell around him, Washington remained untouched.

The British retreated and Washington dashed after them, urging his men forward: "It's a fine fox chase, my boys!" British troops camped in Princeton looked up to see the Continental Army charging toward them. They surrendered. Washington's freezing

General Howe's Dog

Somehow during the Battle of Germantown the American army ended up with General Howe's dog! A gentleman even in war, Washington returned the animal: "Note to Sir William Howe. General Washington's compliments to General Howe does himself the pleasure to return him a Dog, which accidentally fell into his hands, and by the inscription on the Collar appears to belong to General Howe. October 6, 1777."

The Battle of Princeton.

Library of Congress, LC-USZ62-469

soldiers thankfully grabbed British blankets and took charge of hundreds of prisoners. The exhausted army advanced slowly toward Morristown, New Jersey, where they holed up for the winter.

American victories at Trenton and Princeton inspired the patriot cause. Exasperated British generals shook their heads over this ragtag American army that kept slipping away. The Redcoats withdrew and headed back to New York.

At Morristown the army shrank as enlistments ended. Washington begged Congress for supplies. But Congress had granted Washington greater powers when they fled Philadelphia. They expected him to supply

his army by taking or buying what he needed from local farms.

Washington disliked the practice of foraging for food and supplies. The British, too, took what they needed from the population, often without paying even those loyal to the British crown. Citizens resented the army snatching their fences for firewood, their hay for horse fodder, their stores of cabbages and potatoes meant to feed their own families. Washington needed citizens' support–not their anger. "How disgraceful . . . is it," asked Washington, "that the peaceable inhabitants, our countrymen . . . dread our halting among them, even for a night and are happy when they get rid of us?"

By summer 1777 Washington did not know where the British would strike. The British general John Burgoyne had led an army down from Canada and captured the American fort at Ticonderoga. Would Burgoyne now try an invasion of New England? Would he sail down the Hudson to New York? And where would Howe go? At the end of July the British fleet—170 ships strong—sailed out of New York Harbor and turned up in the Chesapeake Bay. Howe planned to unload his troops and march on Philadelphia, the largest American city. The British believed Washington would not let Philadelphia go without a full-out fight. Howe hoped to destroy the American army once and for all.

The Continental Army met the British on September 11, 1777, near Brandywine Creek, Pennsylvania. In the end Washington's troops retreated, swung around, and retreated again. He refused to make a stand that could destroy his army. The British marched easily into Philadelphia. General Howe stationed most of his troops just outside the city at Germantown.

Washington hoped to achieve a surprise strike at Germantown on October 4. At first American victory seemed possible. But as a heavy fog and mist blanketed the battle, everything turned wrong. Troops ran out of ammunition, panicked, and ran. Washington rallied his men and once again slipped away. Howe fortified his position in Philadelphia and settled in for the winter.

Valley Forge

Washington's defeat at Germantown glared all the worse in contrast to news of an American victory in upper New York. Washington had granted General Horatio Gates freedom to act in the north. On October 17, 1777, Gates defeated General Burgoyne at Saratoga. Gates did not hide the fact he wanted Washington's job.

Washington moved his men into winter camp at Valley Forge, Pennsylvania, on December 21. The men built log huts for shelter, 12 men to a hut. By now Washington feared the army faced three choices: starve, dissolve, or scatter to seek food "in the best manner they can." He had nearly 3,000 men unfit for duty "because they are barefoot and otherwise naked." Did the American people think the men were made of stones and would not feel frost and snow?

The arrival of a Prussian (German) officer, Friedrich von Steuben, provided one bright spot during that miserable winter. Von Steuben kept the troops busy, drilling on bayonet use and generally training them into an army.

Washington faced more than cold and hunger that brutal winter. Horatio Gates and several others plotted to replace him. For Washington this nearly was the last straw. But as the plan came to light, members of Congress, citizens, officers, and soldiers rallied to Washington's defense. The plot turned to dust.

Pox-Proofing the Troops

Disease often proved a greater enemy than British musket balls. Smallpox swept through the crowded army camp and nearby Morristown. Washington, who'd had the deadly disease as a young man in Barbados, was immune. To save his army, Washington ordered his troops inoculated against smallpox. Inoculation meant scratching a bit of the dangerous smallpox pus into a healthy person's skin. Hopefully, they'd catch a mild, passing case of the disease and then be safe from ever catching it again.

Washington and Lafayette at Valley Forge.

As the dreadful winter at Valley Forge moved toward spring, Washington's General Orders for March 1, 1778, thanked his soldiers for their suffering and fortitude.

Finally, in May, Washington received good news. France, Great Britain's old enemy, recognized American independence and planned to offer military aid and money. "This is great, 'tis glorious news," he penned his brother John. He ordered muskets and cannon fired in salute, the troops marched on parade, and on signal, "the whole army will Huzza! Long live the King of France" and "To the American States."

Changes took place in the British camp, as well. Sir Henry Clinton replaced Howe as commander in chief. The capture of Philadelphia had won the British little except a winter of parties with Loyalists. Clinton evacuated Philadelphia and headed back to New York.

His Presence Stopped the Retreat

Washington hoped to roar out of Valley Forge and attack the British as they marched to New York. But at a council of war, some of his generals opposed the plan. Charles Lee, who had lost none of his jealousy for Washington as a British prisoner, led the opposition. Within hours, however, three of Washington's most

A Young Frenchman Comes to Help

European officers flocked to Washington's camp. Many had European war experience and felt entitled to high commands and prestige in the infant American army. Others truly believed in the American cause and wanted to help. Washington most liked a modest 20-year-old French aristocrat, the Marquis de Lafayette. (His full name was Marie Joseph Paul Yves Roch Gilbert du Motier.) Lafayette had disobeyed orders from France's King Louis XVI and sailed for America to help the cause. Lafayette proved eager to learn, and willing and ready to follow Washington. He was wounded at the Battle of Brandywine Creek. Later, Washington gave Lafayette command of American troops in Virginia. Lafayette also pressed the French government for more aid to help the Americans. Washington viewed Lafayette as a son, and the two men and their families remained close.

The Marquis de Lafayette in Virginia, 1781.
Library of Congress, LC-USZ62-820

Washington stops the retreat and takes command from Charles Lee at the Battle of Monmouth, June 28, 1778.

trusted generals—Greene, Lafayette, and Anthony Wayne—came to him. They believed Washington should attack. The marching British army stretched out for miles; the baggage wagons alone straggled for nearly a dozen miles. The Americans could at least harass the march and if the opportunity came up, attack. That suited Washington just fine.

Washington offered the command to Lee, who turned him down. Washington then gave Lafayette the job and increased the size of the attacking force. Now that more men were involved Lee claimed his honor demanded he get command even though he still disapproved of Washington's plan. So Lee took charge.

June 28, 1778, dawned hot and muggy near Monmouth Courthouse, New Jersey. Waiting back with his troops Washington heard sounds of battle ahead—and then silence. Had the British escaped? He galloped forward and found the American regiments in retreat, the soldiers confused. Washington left his command with General Greene and dashed ahead to find Lee.

Fury rang in Washington's voice. "What is all this confusion for, and retreat?"

Stunned at the rage on Washington's face, Lee stammered. His orders were disobeyed, said Lee; the ground was too extensive for his troops to cover, and he had never trusted Washington's plan.

Washington listened then exploded: "All this may be very true, sir, but you ought not to have undertaken it unless you intended to go through with it!"

The British surged after the retreating Americans. Washington rallied his men to fight. They battled the British to a standstill in a day-long struggle of heat, dust, and blood, where parched men begged for water. In darkness the British resumed their march to New York. Washington let his exhausted men rest before following.

Lafayette described Washington at the Battle of Monmouth: "General Washington seemed to arrest fortune with one glance. . . . His presence stopped the retreat. . . . I thought then as now that I had never beheld so superb a man."

The British army was not Washington's only problem. He spent hours trying to persuade friends, congressmen, and business leaders that the only way to win the war was for the individual states to pull together. Washington viewed the news that Congress had drawn up Articles of Confederation as a good step. If the states approved, the Articles provided a blueprint for the states to work together.

Unfortunately, the states, used to their own complete power, jealously guarded their rights. Many states did not want their men serving in a national army that might smudge the boundaries of state allegiance. And the states refused to let Congress pass taxes to pay for the war.

Washington noted that after two years, "both armies are brought back to the very point they set out from," in New York. He had kept his come-and-go army in the field to fight the British, and if he hadn't won the war, he had not lost it, either. For the rest of 1778 the armies stayed put.

Meanwhile, Washington rejoiced at news that a French fleet would be available to help fight the British. He desperately needed French ships to strike the British in New York. But the fleet sailed away without bothering to tell Washington where it headed! Most French officers did not hide their disdain for the upstart Americans. "I most devoutly wish that we had not a single foreign officer among us," Washington wrote in frustration, "except the Marquis of Lafayette." Washington spent a few months in Philadelphia meeting with Congress, which had returned to the city when the British pulled out. But Congress had no money for Washington to attack the British—he needed the French fleet and its troops.

A Many-Headed Monster

By 1778 the Continental Army's worst enemy was the American economy. Few people had hard money, meaning gold or silver coins. Congress printed piles of paper money, but with no gold or silver holdings to back it up, the paper bills grew worthless. It required $2,934 in paper to equal $100 in coins. At the same time, prices for everything skyrocketed.

Lady Washington in Camp

Throughout the war, Martha traveled to live with George during the winter encampments. She brought Washington a touch of home and peace, as well as a social life. Other officers' wives and local ladies would join the Washingtons for dinner, conversation, and horse rides. The wife of one Virginia officer wrote to a friend, "Now let me speak of our noble and agreeable commander, for he commands both sexes, one by his excellent skill in military matters, the other by his ability, politeness, and attention." She noted that Martha called George "her Old Man."

Roll a Beeswax Candle

Before electric or gas lights, people relied on candles for light. Candles could be made by dipping a long wick over and over into melted wax. Or the melted wax could be poured into candle molds and left to harden. Rolling a candle from a sheet of beeswax was another method of candlemaking.

Lay the sheet of beeswax on the table. It should be at room temperature, not too cold or too hot. Choose 1 side of the beeswax sheet and cut your wick 1 inch longer than that side. Press the wick into the edge of the beeswax, then roll the edge over the wick, sealing it into the wax.

Carefully begin rolling the beeswax sheet around the wick. Try to keep the candle tight and the edges even. At the end, gently press the wax edge into the candle to seal it. If your candle is too fat to fit into your candlestick, use the warmth of your hand to gently squeeze and stretch the bottom of the candle to fit into a candleholder.

Materials

Sheet of beeswax (from a craft store)
String, for the wick
Scissors
Ruler
Candleholder

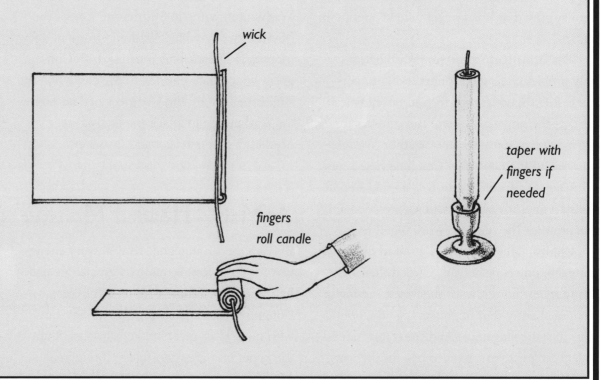

wick

fingers roll candle

taper with fingers if needed

Merchants and farmers demanded coins for their goods. Those who had coins used them, making other people's paper bills even more worthless. Soldiers, paid in paper money, earned only a fraction of what they'd been promised when they joined up. Many soldiers had not been paid at all–for months.

Congress could not afford to feed or clothe the soldiers, either. Sometimes the soldiers faced five or six days without bread or meat. The states, unwilling to lose power to Congress, let the troubles worsen daily. Washington described the situation: Congress made a request to the states. One state helped, one state ignored the request, and another would give only half.

The situation left Washington raw with frustration. He urged the states to set up a Congress with powers "in all matters relative to the great purposes of war and of general concern by which the states unitedly are affected." If not, Washington feared, "We are attempting an impossibility and very soon shall become (if it is not already the case) a many-headed monster . . . that never will or can steer to the same point."

The Situation Darkens

During 1779 Washington strengthened his positions around the British in New York. Again, he itched for action. If he could only strike the British in New York, he might be able to end the war.

The Americans set up winter quarters again at Morristown. More than 20 snowstorms battered the camp. Men, pinched with hunger, gnawed tree bark and roasted shoe leather. Officers killed a dog and ate it. Washington begged Congress for more money and better supply systems. He greatly feared that his soldiers, who risked their lives in return for misery, might mutiny.

Bad news flooded Washington's headquarters. The American army in the south had lost Charleston, South Carolina, to the British. The Redcoats had captured 2,500 Continental soldiers and 2,000 militiamen. Washington sent General Gates south, but the British roundly defeated Gates at the Battle of Camden, on August 16, 1780. Washington sent his trusted friend Nathanael Greene to command the southern army. Then a ray of good news arrived: a French army was coming. Washington believed–at last!–he could strike New York and perhaps end the war with an American victory.

Rochambeau

The French army commanded by the Count de Rochambeau set up camp in Rhode Island in July. Rochambeau thought Washington foolish to believe he could attack New York. The

Betrayed!

On his return from meeting Rochambeau, Washington visited the American fort at West Point overlooking the Hudson River. He looked forward to seeing his hard-fighting general, Benedict Arnold, the commander of the post. Instead, Arnold was nowhere to be found and a packet of papers revealed he'd gone over to the British side. Aides described Washington trembling with shock and rage, the papers proving Arnold's treachery scattered about the floor. "Arnold has betrayed us! Whom can we trust now?" he cried.

The Americans captured British major John Andre, Arnold's accomplice. The Americans couldn't help but like the gentlemanly young British officer. Washington offered to trade Andre for Arnold. But British Commander Clinton turned him down. Clinton still hoped to lure other American officers to act as spies and change sides. The British gave Arnold command of 1,500 men to raid the Virginia countryside. Washington regretfully ordered Andre hanged as a spy.

An unflattering British cartoon from 1780 shows Rochambeau inspecting his troops.

Library of Congress, LC-USZ62-1518

Mutiny!

The Americans' distress sank lower over the winter of 1780–81. Washington spent his own money to buy food for his staff. Then, in January 1781, he received news he'd long been dreading: more than 2,000 Pennsylvania troops at Morristown had mutinied, killing one officer, before marching on Congress in Philadelphia to present their demands. Washington feared other troops would join the mutiny. From New York headquarters he sent word warning Congress not to flee. Congress promised the mutineers cash bounties and discharged nearly half the soldiers.

Then 200 New Jersey troops marched on the state capital. The mutineers surrendered to handpicked troops sent by Washington. He ordered several mutineers shot as a warning to others, for liberty could not survive with "armed soldiers dictating terms to their country." Washington knew the financial crisis stood at the bottom of his mutinous troops' actions. "We are at the end of our tether," he wrote. "Now or never, our deliverance must come."

Campaign in the Chesapeake

In the spring of 1781, while Washington again pushed Rochambeau to strike New York, word

Frenchman reported that Washington had only 3,000 men. "Send us troops, ships, and money," Rochambeau wrote back to France, "but do not depend on these people nor upon their means: they have neither money nor credit; their means of resistance are only momentary and called forth when they are attacked."

Washington traveled to meet Rochambeau in September 1780 and immediately brought up strategies to take New York. Rochambeau interrupted. How many men could the Americans raise to fight? Washington admitted he could not say due to the money crunch the army faced. Rochambeau discouraged further discussions. Washington left the meeting depressed—five years of war and no end in sight.

Write with a Quill Pen

Washington spent hours writing to Congress and the state governments giving news and seeking aid. He also wrote to family and friends. And each letter, many pages and pages long, was written with a quill feather pen dipped in ink. Most people owned a penknife to keep their quills sharp and a supply of quills to make fresh pens.

Materials

Large feather (from a craft store); turkey or goose works best
Scissors
Bottle of colored ink

Take the scissors and snip the feather quill (the center of the feather) to make a point, as shown. Dip the quill into ink, tapping off the excess against the side of the ink bottle. The hollow center of the quill will hold some ink so you can write. When the ink runs out, dip your pen again. When the pen grows dull, cut a new point. Practice until you can write clearly with the quill pen!

feather

quill

cut point with scissors

arrived that changed his plans. A French fleet under the Count de Grasse would sail from the West Indies to the Chesapeake Bay. Washington's attention turned toward Virginia.

In July the French and American armies joined camps on the Hudson. American soldiers in faded, patched uniforms, some with only ragged blankets tied about their shoulders, must have stared at the well-fed French soldiers' spotless uniforms dripping with gold braid and the plumes upon their hats. Washington entertained 30 French officers only to hear complaints about his watery coffee, plain vinegar on the lettuce, and only one plate of food. That Washington and his officers sat and talked like old friends, telling jokes and eating hickory nuts, further amazed the French.

The man who interpreted for Washington and Rochambeau noted, "It is incredible that soldiers composed of men of every age, even children of 15, of whites and blacks, almost naked, unpaid, and rather poorly fed, can march so well and stand fire so steadfastly." He credited Washington's calm: "He is certainly admirable as the leader of his army, in which everyone regards him as his father and friend."

De Grasse would reach the Chesapeake Bay in the first week of September and leave in mid-October. The French and American armies needed to hurry. Every detail worried Washington. What if storms or the British fleet drove de Grasse off? The long march would use most of Washington's meager resources to

Mount Vernon Threatened

Washington learned that the British ship *Savage* had sailed up the Potomac and threatened Mount Vernon. His cousin Lund, managing the estate for Washington, saved the house by giving supplies to the British. Lund's actions upset Washington. He wrote to his cousin he would rather have heard that Mount Vernon had burned when Lund scorned the British demand of supplies.

Cornwallis's army surrenders to Washington at Yorktown, Virginia.
Library of Congress, LC-USZ62-26632

feed his troops. And what if the British general in Virginia, Cornwallis, escaped before the French and Americans arrived?

Washington pretended New York remained the target. He spread false reports for British spies. He sent men to prepare a major army camp outside New York. The British remained unaware that the main armies had slipped away and crossed the Delaware, planning to travel down the river and into the Chesapeake.

On September 5, 1781, Rochambeau and his staff, drifting down the Delaware River, spied a tall man in uniform running along the shore. He jumped up and down and joyfully waved both his hat and his handkerchief. It was George Washington–de Grasse had safely arrived! He'd fought off a British fleet and now blocked the entrance to the Chesapeake Bay from the sea.

As the army sped south, Washington made a quick detour to Mount Vernon, his first visit home since April 1775. Here he and Rochambeau planned the siege of Yorktown.

The World Turned Upside Down

Cornwallis did not escape. At Yorktown, Virginia, on September 28, the French and American armies trapped Cornwallis with his back to the water. The British hunkered behind earthwork defenses. The Americans and French, with pickaxes and shovels, dug a series of trenches circling the British position. Cannon fire thundered day and night, the midnight sky crisscrossed by the screaming missiles' flaming tails. Washington himself fired the first shot.

On October 14 the allies stormed two British strongholds called Redoubts 9 and 10. They drove back a British counterattack and dug a new line closer to the British. Three days later, American soldiers, deafened by the constant shelling, spied a drummer boy on top of the battered British line. A white flag followed.

A General's Epaulets

From his childhood George Washington loved designing military uniforms. No uniform was complete without decorative epaulets on the shoulders.

Materials

Cardboard or poster board

Scissors

Ruler

Quilt batting (available at craft stores)

12-inch-wide square of felt in your favorite color

Glue

Double-stick tape

Gold braid with fringe

Sequins, stars, etc.

Cut the cardboard/poster board into two rectangles, about 2 inches by 4 inches. Cut the batting into two rectangles the same size as the cardboard. Cut the felt into two rectangles, 1 inch bigger all the way around (4 inches by 6 inches) than the batting and cardboard. Glue the batting to the top of the cardboard. Wrap the felt around the cardboard, completely covering the batting, and glue or double-stick tape the edges to the back of the cardboard. Lay the gold braid fringe around the edges of your epaulet on the front (felt-covered) side and cut it to fit. Glue or double-stick tape the fringe in place. Glue on sequins or stars. Attach the epaulet to your shoulders with double-stick tape.

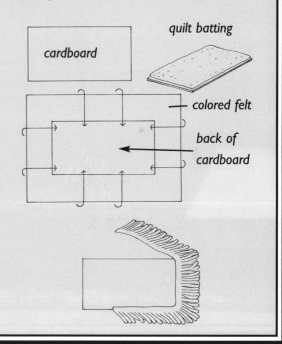

quilt batting

cardboard

colored felt

back of cardboard

Cornwallis sent Washington a message proposing a truce "to settle terms for surrender."

Cornwallis insisted he was too sick to attend the surrender on October 19. He sent one of his generals to hand over his sword. The British officer tried to hand the sword to a French officer instead of Washington. The notes of the British marching song "The World Turned Upside Down" filled the air, and so it must have seemed to the British as they marched between long lines of French and ragged Continental soldiers. Said one Continental man, the scene "was too pleasing to an American."

Cornwallis surrendered over 7,000 soldiers, 840 sailors, 250 cannon, and thousands of guns. But it was only part of British military might in North America. De Grasse sailed back to the Indies and the British navy again controlled American waters. The war continued.

Goaded by a Thousand Stings

A month after Yorktown, Washington's family suffered a personal loss when Martha's son Jacky became ill and died. He left a widow and four young children.

Washington spent four months trying to wring pay and supplies from Congress. But if Washington bemoaned the "unpromising state of our affairs," the British also found the situation unpromising. Parliament voted to end the costly war against their former colonies. The new British commander in chief, Sir Guy Carleton, informed Washington that peace negotiations had started in Paris.

Washington had outlasted four British commanders. The war with Britain might have been winding down, but Washington faced a new menace. The American Revolution had reached a crisis point, a crisis with its own soldiers.

Many of his officers had not been paid in years. Instead of keeping the troops in line, his officers now led the angry complaints. No one believed Congress could keep its promise of awarding pensions to those who had fought. Heavily in debt, officers and men felt no gratitude from their fellow citizens. "I am in rags," wrote one soldier, "and all this for my cowardly countrymen [who] hold their Purse Strings . . . rather than part with a Dollar to their Army." Washington knew the breaking point loomed near, the men "goaded by a thousand stings . . . soured by . . . the ingratitude of the public."

An anonymous letter circulated through the army camp at Newburgh, New York. The letter urged the soldiers not to go home, but instead to turn their weapons against the new nation until they received justice. It called for a meeting of officers to discuss the situation.

With tempers already stressed, Washington feared the letter would incite the men toward violence. On March 15, 1783, Washington slipped into the meeting. He looked around the room at men who had suffered and stood by him for years. Now they regarded him with anger and distrust.

Washington talked about his love for his soldiers. He reminded them he had been their companion in every misery. He pleaded for calm. He pleaded they not abandon "our Country in the extremest hour of her distress. . . . My God! What can this writer have in view, by recommending such measures." He pleaded with the soldiers not to "open the flood gates of civil discord, and deluge our rising empire in blood."

Their silence and stony faces showed he had not convinced them. They did not trust him. He fumbled in his pocket for a note of encouragement he'd received from a congressman. For a moment Washington looked confused. Then he pulled out a pair of glasses. No one but his closest advisors had seen the general wear his spectacles.

He cleared his throat. "Gentlemen, you will permit me to put on my spectacles, for I have not only grown gray but almost blind in the service of my country."

This quiet statement forced its way straight to the heart. Suddenly, men were blinking back tears. Once again, Washington found a way to lead his men. To Congress he angrily wrote that if they did not pay the troops, "I shall have learned what ingratitude is; then I shall have realized a tale which will embitter every moment of my future life!" But Congress had no money.

General Orders, April 18, 1783

It was just another morning. Shoulder to shoulder the men lined up to hear orders read. But what words they heard! George Washington announced the end of hostilities "between the United States of America and the King of Great Britain."

The end to the war, Washington promised them, "opens the prospect to a more splendid scene, and, like another morning star, promises the approach of a brighter day." He congratulated the troops for their dignity, for their part in establishing "Freedom . . . on the broad basis of Independency." They had "assisted in protecting the rights of human nature and established an asylum for the poor and oppressed of all nations and religions." Five months later, on September 3, 1783, the peace treaty ending the American Revolution was officially signed.

Washington sent a letter to the states urging them to strengthen the Articles of Confederation (adopted in 1781) and form a central government with enough power to meet the

A Stronger Government

To his brother John, Washington confided his doubts that the states would carry through on setting up a strong central government. He wondered why people feared granting power to the Congress. "For Heavens sake who are Congress? Are they not the Creatures of the People? . . . . Where then can be the danger of giving them such Powers as are adequate to the great ends of Government?"

Washington leads his troops into New York City as the British leave, November 25, 1783.

needs of the new nation. And the nation owed the soldiers for their blood and suffering. "It is therefore more than a common debt, it is a debt of honour," Washington wrote.

Congress disbanded the troops, except a small force guarding the British still camped in New York. As the British finally left on November 25, 1783, the American army, with Washington at the head, entered the city. A few days later Washington bid an emotional farewell to his officers, then rode to Annapolis, Maryland, where Congress was meeting. For many, George Washington stood as a living symbol of the American Revolution. Grateful crowds cheered him on his way south.

On December 23, 1783, his hands and voice trembling, Washington resigned his military commission before Congress. All around him, men and women wept. In stepping aside, he presented the nation his greatest gift. He would not use his popularity, or his army, to gain power for himself. Washington's actions assured that the new nation would be a free republic, not a monarchy under a new King George as some had feared. Thomas Jefferson would later write about Washington, "The moderation and virtue of a single character probably prevented the Revolution from being closed, as most others have been, by a subversion of that liberty it was intended to establish."

On Christmas Eve, Washington stepped through his own front door at Mount Vernon. "I am become a private citizen on the banks of the Potomac," he wrote to Lafayette. "Envious of none, I am determined to be pleased with all, & this my dear friend, being the order of my march, I will move gently down the stream of life until I sleep with my fathers."

On December 4, 1783, at Fraunces Tavern in New York, Washington hugged each of his officers as he bid them farewell.

Lafayette and Washington at Mount Vernon.

5

"Summoned by My Country"

uffled against the January wind, George Washington walked the grounds of Mount Vernon. Trees planted by his own hands had grown tall in the nearly nine years since he'd left. He felt time passing, running out. His farms needed work. He faced a financial mess; like so many others, he'd lost money during the war. Everything required his attention.

Washington fought melancholy with action. He rose early and, in his nightshirt, padded down the private back staircase to his study. Here he shaved, dressed, and tied his long hair back with a ribbon. He handled

Mount Vernon.

The "large dining room" at Mount Vernon, which Washington finished after the war.

Courtesy of the Mount Vernon Ladies' Association

household duties before eating three corn cakes dripping butter and honey, and three cups of tea without cream.

No detail of house or farm escaped his notice. Mount Vernon bustled like a small city. Down one lane, in a neat row, stood a spinning house, a smokehouse, stables and barns, a coach house, and a laundry house, all worked by slaves. Washington experimented with grasses for grazing cows. He bred sheep and mules. He rotated his crops and tested fertilizers to improve his soil. He began decorating the two-story entertaining room he'd planned before the war.

Relatives moved into Mount Vernon, including Martha's two youngest grandchildren, three-year-old George Washington Parke Custis, called Wash, and five-year-old Eleanor Parke Custis, called Nelly. Martha's niece, Fanny Bassett, arrived as well. So did George's niece, Harriott, the daughter of his dead brother Samuel.

Hundreds of friends and curious strangers graced Washington's doorstep. Washington felt obliged to entertain each person. Some unpacked and stayed for weeks, crammed into Mount Vernon's bedrooms.

It cost Washington a fortune to feed this hoard of guests. The day's main meal–dinner–was served at three in the afternoon. If Washington liked the guests he'd sit and chat. People commented how he smiled a great deal and laughed. At six o'clock the family enjoyed tea. But unless the guests were close friends, Washington usually did not re-appear later for supper, served around the time George went to bed–nine o'clock!

Other close friends had left Virginia before the Revolution. George William and Sally Fairfax were far away in London, and Washington heard that Belvoir had burned during the war. For nearly a year he could not bring himself to visit the house. But finally he rode over and walked among the blackened rubbish piled around him. He wrote to George William and Sally that he'd fled from the scene where "the happiest moments of my life had been spent."

Design a Room

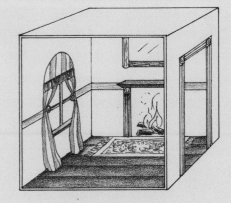

George Washington constantly planned improvements for Mount Vernon, even while he was away during the American Revolution and, later, his presidency. He spent time on every detail, choosing everything from fireplace designs to the colors for the walls. The family dining room and the large dining room at Mount Vernon were both painted bright shades of green!

Adult supervision required

Materials

Sturdy cardboard box at least 12 inches by 12 inches (bigger is better!)

Spray paint in the main color you wish to paint your room

Craft knife with retractable blade

Paints

Brushes

Details from a craft shop, such as yarn, craft sticks, moldings, etc.

Take the box outdoors and spray paint the inside. With adult help, use a craft knife to cut doorways and windows into your room. Paint the floor to look like wood or a black-and-white tile checkerboard.

If you'd like, paint in a fireplace. Glue architectural details like ceiling moldings or chair rails onto the walls. Paint a wallpaper design. Weave a rug. Make a large mirror by framing a piece of aluminum foil with craft sticks painted gold or silver. Create a painting to hang on the wall.

Make a Plaster Decoration in Sand

Beautiful plasterwork decorates the ceiling and walls of Mount Vernon's two-story large dining room. The room is elegant, but Washington included farm images like scythes, wheat, plows, and shovels in his designs.

Create your own plaster design to hang on your wall.

Adult supervision required

Materials

Old newspapers

Disposable foil
    roasting pan,
    about 3 inches
    deep

Play sand

Water

Pencil

Small can

Marbles, shells, and
    other small
    decorative objects

Chicken wire

Wire cutter

Bag of plaster

Plastic paint bucket

Wire coat hanger

Paint stirrer

Measuring cup

Spread the newspaper on a table to work on. Add about 2 inches of sand to the foil roasting pan. Dampen the sand with water and stir it around with the paint stirrer. Pat the sand down smooth and even. Make a design in the sand. You can draw lines and swirls with the end of a pencil. You can push circles into the sand with a small can. Press in marbles, shells, or any other small decorative objects. These objects can be left in the sand and will show in the final sandcasting.

With adult help, cut a piece of chicken wire to fit inside the roasting pan—keep this handy for later. Follow the directions on the plaster packaging to mix the dry plaster with water in the plastic paint bucket. Slowly pour about half of the plaster over the sand, making sure the plaster fills your design in the sand. To help support your sandcasting, place the chicken wire on top of the plaster. Pour the rest of the plaster over the chicken wire and fill the roasting pan.

With adult help, cut a piece of the wire coat hanger and bend it like an upside-down block *U*, as shown. Put the coat hanger *U* into the plaster along the top edge. This will let you hang your sandcasting.

Let the plaster set and dry. When the plaster is completely dried, carefully lift it out of the roasting pan. Brush off the sand or rinse the sandcasting with a garden hose; some sand will remain embedded. Your design should show in the plaster! Now—hang your plaster work up!

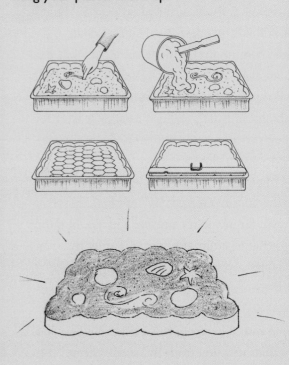

One welcomed guest was Lafayette, shown leaving Mount Vernon after a visit in 1784.
Library of Congress, LC-USZ62-2264

Artists descended on Mount Vernon to paint and sculpt the famous man. Washington felt uncomfortable being stared at, studied, and posed, but wrote to a friend that he was getting used to it. In October 1785 the famous French sculptor Jean-Antoine Houdon arrived at Mount Vernon. Over the course of two weeks he studied Washington, took careful measurements of his subject, and made a plaster life mask of George's face. As Houdon slathered plaster on Washington's face, six-year-old Nelly walked past the door. She saw her white-faced grandfather laid out on a table covered to the chin with a sheet. Poor Nelly thought her grandfather had died! The Washington family believed Houdon's sculpture the most true to the real man.

A deluge of letters and requests also rained down on Mount Vernon. Washington hired a secretary, Mr. Tobias Lear, to help him answer them. Lear became part of the family and later would write about Washington, "I have never found a single thing that could lessen my respect for him."

One Visitor's Story

Elkanah Watson visited Mount Vernon in January 1785. He carried a letter of introduction from Washington's friend Nathanael Greene. Though Watson suffered with a bad cold he spent the evening talking with Washington, amazed that the famous man offered him so much attention. Washington urged various cough medicines on Watson, but Watson declined. He would just go to bed. But once he lay down his cough worsened. He heard the door quietly open. Watson sat up and peered through the bed curtains. With astonishment he saw Washington himself at the bedside holding a cup of steaming tea for Watson's cough.

Shays's Rebellion

Most states yawned at the notion of a convention to strengthen the Articles of Confederation, until an event in late 1786 helped change their point of view. Settlers in Massachusetts could not scrape together cash to pay off their debts. Many lost their farms or landed in debtor's prison. Furious mobs led by Daniel Shays marched through Massachusetts.

Washington feared for the country. He viewed Shays's Rebellion as "a call for decision." If Shays's followers had real grievances, Washington believed they should be fixed or at least acknowledged. If not, "employ the force of the government against them at once."

But that was the problem. People realized the government had little power to stop a rebellion. The country hung by a thread with no government really in charge. What if Shays's Rebellion spread to other states?

In the end, the Massachusetts governor, with money raised by Boston bankers, hired a militia to face down the rebels. Shays's Rebellion fizzled. But it left people thinking a convention to strengthen the national government was not such a bad idea.

The Growing Frontier

Washington turned to another passion—western lands. In September 1784 he crossed the mountains to visit the frontier. The area around the Forks of the Ohio, where he'd stood as a young man alone in the wilderness, now teemed with settlers. Washington felt the United States must quickly capture the loyalty of these frontier citizens before Spain or Great Britain came wooing. Great Britain, a presence in Canada and the Great Lakes region, stirred up trouble in the West. And Spain controlled the huge Louisiana Territory and the important Mississippi River.

Trade provided one way to cement the bonds between East and West. Settlers needed an easy way to ship their goods back to eastern states, and that meant river travel. Washington helped charter the Potomac Company. He created a plan to join western rivers to the Potomac, helped by new canals and short wagon routes. Washington believed a water system that brought "navigation almost to every man's door" would strengthen American bonds and improve the economy. But it would also require cooperation among rival states— and he knew how difficult that could be.

Washington hosted a meeting at Mount Vernon for delegates from Maryland and Virginia to settle an argument over fishing rights. This first step grew into the September 1786 Annapolis Convention, where several states discussed "commercial cooperation." Washington, who'd sworn himself finished with public life, did not attend the Annapolis Convention. But he let people know he hoped the convention might discuss government as well as economics. Only five states sent delegates, but they made a bold decision. They called for a new meeting in Philadelphia to discuss changes to the Articles of Confederation.

Washington wholeheartedly approved. If Congress continued to lack real power "we never shall establish a National Character," he wrote, "or be considered on a respectable footing by the powers of Europe." The country could not continue as "one Nation today, & thirteen tomorrow—who will treat with us on such terms?" In Washington's mind, the confederation had become "little more than an empty sound." But he envisioned a great future for his country. "We have it in our power to be one of the most respectable Nations upon Earth," Washington insisted, but only "if we would pursue a wise, Just, & liberal policy towards one another."

Fellow Virginians urged Washington to lead their delegates at the convention. As usual, Washington debated what to do. He had announced he was finished with public life.

But one reason tipped the balance and sent Washington to Philadelphia. This convention offered the best hope of finishing the job started by the war. His country needed strength and stability to survive. "Let us look

Cast a Plaster Life Mask

More than once Washington lay still while a sculptor smeared his face with plaster to create a life mask. Your face will be the one cast in this activity.

Adult supervision required

Materials

Roll of plaster gauze (from a craft store)

Scissors

Ruler

Drinking straw

Measuring cup

Bowl

Plaster of paris

Old shirt, or old sheet or towel

Wide cloth headband

Petroleum jelly (like Vaseline)

Table or comfortable chair

Pillow covered with old sheet or towel

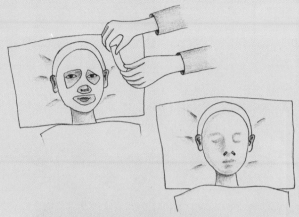

Your adult assistant (or two assistants) should cut the gauze strips into pieces 3 or 4 inches long and 1 inch wide, and cut several small pieces to use around your nostrils. Snip the drinking straw into two pieces 2 inches long. Put ½ cup of warm water into a bowl. Mix in about ⅓ cup of plaster of paris.

Wear an old T-shirt or cover yourself up to the shoulders with an old sheet or towel. Use the headband to hold all your hair back; you don't want the plaster to stick to it. Rub a good coat of petroleum jelly all over your face and onto your hairline. Rub it over your eyes (keep them closed!) and lips, too. Place the pieces of drinking straw gently in your nostrils to breathe through. Get comfortable. You can lie on a table with your head on a pillow, but cover the pillow with an old towel or sheet. Close your eyes and breathe slowly through the straws. This will feel weird, but there is nothing to worry about, so relax.

Your helper should then dip the strips into the water/plaster mixture one at a time and apply them to your face. Start along the edges of the face and under the jaw. The edges of the gauze should overlap and your helper should smooth them into your face with his or her fingers. Keep covering the rest of the face, leaving the eyes and mouth for last. Have your helper warn you when he or she is going to cover your eyes and mouth. Put strips around the nostrils, allowing you to breathe freely through the straws.

Do a second layer, and maybe three layers around the edges and under your jaw. Smooth it out as much as possible. Keep your face very still. Listen to music or have someone read to you or talk to you. But whatever you do, don't move your face! Let the plaster set for about 10 to 15 minutes. Feel if it has hardened everywhere.

Use both hands to gently pull the cast down and away from the face—it may take a little time to work it free. Move your mouth and face around to help. Take your time.

Clean up your face. Let the cast dry completely.

beyond the present period," he wrote to James Madison. "No morn ever dawned more favourable than ours did–and no day was more clouded than the present!"

A New Constitution

All 13 states except Rhode Island sent delegates to Philadelphia. Within days the delegates made a radical decision: scrap the Articles of Confederation and start fresh. They'd write a new constitution establishing "a national government . . . consisting of a Supreme legislative, executive, and judiciary."

Washington hoped everyone might find common ground for agreement. But most delegates worried how a new constitution would affect their own state and region. Men from different sections regarded one another with distrust. Most delegates had never visited other areas of the country. Even Washington had never stepped north of Boston or south of Virginia.

How were 55 people going to agree on something as important as a new government? They did agree on one point. The delegates unanimously elected Washington president of the Constitutional Convention. Throughout the debates he sat behind a table at the front of the room. For the sake of order he stayed out of the often-heated debates. However, his face mirrored his emotions for all to see.

Washington presides over the Constitutional Convention in Philadelphia, 1787.
Library of Congress, LC-USZ62-92869

From May to September the delegates hammered out which powers should go to the states and which to the central, or "federal," government. Local matters belonged to the states. Issues affecting the whole nation, like war, treaties, and trade, belonged to the federal government. But what powers should the new government have to tax? Did they risk the same tyranny, with a strong central government, as

they'd known under Great Britain? But without a strong government the new nation lay at the mercy of rebellions and anarchy.

Philadelphia's steamy weather mirrored the testy debates inside the chamber. The hottest issue loomed between the larger, more populous states and the smaller states. A state like Virginia had 15 times the population of a state like Delaware. How would each be represented in the legislative branch? If larger states were given more votes because they had more citizens, they could always push their interests over the smaller states. Small states wanted each state to hold an equal vote.

After wrangling and threats the delegates reached a compromise: the legislature would have two "houses." Members would be elected to the House of Representatives based on a state's population. But each state would elect just two senators. In the Senate, each state had an equal vote.

Intense arguments over slavery ended in a compromise: a slave would count as three-fifths of a human being when a state's population was counted, and Congress would not ban the slave trade for at least 20 years.

The new Constitution called for an executive, or president. Many feared granting power to one man as if he were a king. The convention even considered an executive branch with three men. As discussions wore on, people glanced at the man seated at the front of the room. A delegate from South Carolina noted, "Many of the members . . . shaped their Ideas of the Powers to be given to a President by their opinions of his [Washington's] Virtues."

On September 17, 1787, 39 delegates from 12 states stepped forward and signed the new Constitution. The new government with three branches, each with checks and balances on the others, now needed to be ratified (approved) by 9 of the 13 states to go into effect.

Battle lines quickly appeared in each state. Pamphlets for and against the Constitution flew off the presses. Some of the most important writings supporting the Constitution were the *Federalist Papers*, written by Alexander Hamilton, James Madison, and John Jay. Washington read the pamphlets and followed the debates from Mount Vernon. He wrote to an Irish acquaintance, "We exhibit at present the . . . astonishing spectacle of a whole people deliberating calmly on what form of government will be most conducive to their happiness."

Few people doubted the nation's first president would be George Washington. That calmed some fears that a strong executive might turn himself into an American king. Madison wrote to Thomas Jefferson about Washington, "Be assured, his influence carried this government."

Washington felt no government ever had so many checks to prevent a slide into oppression. "The power under the Constitution will always be with the people," he wrote to his nephew Bushrod. Washington wrote to fellow Virginian Patrick Henry, "I wish the Constitution which is offered had been more perfect but I sincerely believe it is the best that could be obtained at this time, and, as a constitutional door is open to amendment, . . .the adoption of it . . . is in my opinion, desirable." Several states needed the promise of added amendments, in a Bill of Rights that ensured citizens' liberties. Washington urged that a Bill

of Rights be added to gather the states behind the new government.

In late June 1788 Washington rejoiced when the 9th and 10th states–New Hampshire and Virginia–ratified the Constitution. Now voters had to elect representatives for the first Congress. Washington crossed his fingers that people would pick men friendly toward the new government to set it soundly on its feet.

President!

Electors in each state would gather to choose the nation's first president. Each state decided how to pick their electors. In New Hampshire the state legislature appointed the electors. In New Jersey the governor and his council named the electors. In Pennsylvania all voters picked the electors.

Each elector had two votes. On February 4, 1789, each of the 69 electors cast one vote for George Washington for president of the United States. John Adams of Massachusetts, a lawyer and brilliant political thinker, received 34 of the electors' remaining votes, the second-highest total. That made Adams the vice president. The two men were not close, however. Washington did seek Adams's advice, but their cool relationship pushed the vice president's role into the background, where it remained for centuries.

Build a Weather Vane

In 1787 Washington added a final touch to Mount Vernon: a weather vane in the shape of a dove. Washington's dove, with its wings spread in flight, held an olive branch in its beak, symbolizing peace. The Mount Vernon weather vane had arrows that showed what direction the wind was blowing.

Adult supervision required

Materials

Cardboard, about 16 inches long and
    14 inches high
Pen
Craft knife with retractable blade
2 heavy washers
Tape
½-inch dowel rod
Can of gold metallic spray paint
Plastic bottle, such as a water bottle or
    soda pop bottle
Sand
Newspaper

Decide on the design of your weather vane, and draw it on the cardboard. With adult help, use a craft knife to cut out the shape. Figure out which end of the weather vane you would like to point into the wind. Somewhere near that end, tape the two washers, one on each side of the cardboard.

With your thumb and index finger, loosely hold the weather vane from the top edge. Change its position in your hand until it balances. When it does, you should be holding it closer to the front end (nearer to the washers) than the back end. Mark where you are holding the weather vane with a pen. Just below the mark you made, tape the dowel rod securely to the weather vane, pointing down, as shown.

Take the weather vane and bottle outside. Spray paint everything gold (including the washers and dowel rod); be sure to spray them on all sides. Let everything dry.

Using a newspaper funnel, fill the bottle ¾ full with sand. Stick the dowel rod into the sand, but not to deep. Your decorative weather vane should spin when tapped. When it's windy, it should point into the wind.

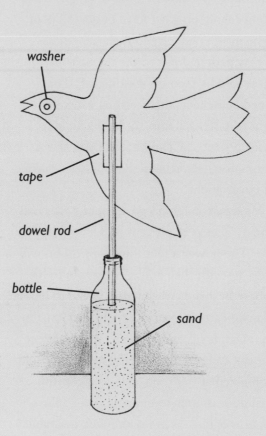

washer

tape

dowel rod

bottle

sand

Standing in the large dining room at Mount Vernon on April 14, Washington received word of his election. Washington set weighty goals for his new job. He had to secure the people's loyalty to the new government. He hoped to ease regional differences. And for the newborn government to work, he needed to spread a spirit of compromise among government branches. He also needed to tackle the nation's money troubles. The United States was a nation of farmers, but Washington hoped to encourage manufacturing, as well. A country could not be strong if they had to buy everything from foreign powers.

"I consider myself," Washington wrote, "entering upon an unexplored field, enveloped on every side with clouds & darkness." Doubts about his "political skills" gnawed at him. As servants loaded his luggage into wagons for the trip to New York City, the new nation's temporary capital, Washington's feelings were "not unlike those of a culprit who's going to the place of his execution."

All along Washington's route people clogged the roads to cheer and celebrate. Riders chased his carriage. People shoved and pushed and reached out to touch him. He stopped for parades and formal dinners in towns small and large. Beneath the cheers Washington sensed a frenzy that panicked him even more. "So much is expected," he wrote, and yet "so many untoward circumstances may intervene, in such a new and critical situa-tion." How could he live up to people's expectations? So much–whether the government would succeed or fail–depended on him. He wrote to his old wartime friend Henry Knox that all he could really promise was to serve with honesty and firmness.

Washington entered New York by boat, escorted by decorated ships and barges sporting brilliant banners and flags that snapped overhead. Crowds lined the wharf. Music and song, cannon thunder and cheers, soared on the April skies. On April 30, 1789, standing on the balcony of Federal Hall in New York City, George Washington was sworn in as president. He wore a new suit of brown velvet sewn from cloth made in America.

"I was summoned by my Country, whose voice I can never hear but with veneration and

Washington arrives in New York City for his inauguration as the first president of the United States.
Library of Congress, LC-USZ62-340

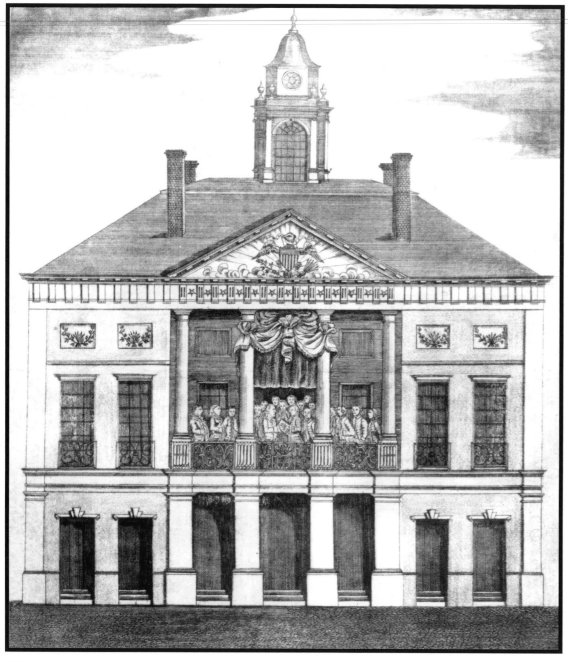

Washington takes the oath of office at Federal Hall, April 30, 1789, in this 1792 print.

Library of Congress, LC-USZ62-126500

love," he told the crowd. As he spoke, Washington shifted his paper from hand to hand, then hooked the fingers of his left hand into his breeches pocket. He asked Providence to help the people find happiness in this "government instituted by themselves." Witnesses noted Washington appeared almost sad. He knew "the preservation of the sacred fire of liberty and the destiny of the republican model of government are . . . staked on the experiment entrusted to the hands of the American people." Fisher Ames, a famous orator, commented that in his simply spoken speech Washington's "power over the heart was never greater."

Martha, Nelly, and Wash arrived in New York in May, but the stress of the job only seemed to grow for Washington. "Few . . . can realize the difficult and delicate part which a man in my situation has to act," he wrote. "I walk on untrodden ground. There is scarcely any part of my conduct which may not hereafter be drawn into precedent."

Not surprisingly, the country's first major crisis centered on Washington's health. His doctors operated on a swelling abscess in his left leg. No anesthesia numbed the pain of surgery. As Washington lay ill, servants scattered straw over the sidewalks to muffle the sound of footsteps. They roped the streets off to carriages. Slowly Washington improved, but it was 40 days before he returned to his desk. Washington believed stress, and a schedule so packed he could not have regular exercise, contributed to his poor health.

Setting Up the Government

One job Washington considered "most difficult & delicate" was choosing heads for the different government departments approved by Congress, what we would call his "cabinet" today. Washington named Henry Knox his secretary of war. Alexander Hamilton, a Washington aide during the war, served as secretary of the treasury. In 1790 Thomas Jefferson accepted the post of secretary of state. Washington believed he'd gathered a strong and trusted group to advise him and build the new government.

Washington usually had his advisors give their opinions and ideas in writing. Sometimes he listened to them discuss an issue, then made his decision. He rarely entered the debate himself. Once he'd made up his mind, Washington figured everyone would accept it.

Washington wondered if he should communicate with Congress in person or in writing. As he needed the Senate's approval for treaties, Washington decided he'd meet with the senators face to face. He went to the Senate chamber to hear debate over a treaty with the Creek Indians. But the debate seemed more like bickering to Washington. He left the chamber frustrated at the senators' time-wasting. In the future, he'd communicate his ideas mostly in writing.

As the first session of Congress ended in late summer 1789, Washington breathed a sigh of relief. Ten new amendments—the Bill of Rights—had been adopted and sent to the states for ratification. Congress had confirmed a chief justice, John Jay, and five other judges for the Supreme Court. The government was, indeed, up and running.

Alexander Hamilton, Washington's first secretary of the treasury.

Library of Congress, LC-USZ62-125560

An Impartial Judge

Unlike later presidents, Washington was not the leader of a political party. In fact, Washington believed the president should be above such things. He believed his main job lay in protecting the U.S. Constitution. He should act as an impartial judge. Adams noted that Washington "seeks information from all quarters and judges more independently than any man I ever knew."

The Death of a Parent

Around the same time Congress adjourned, Washington learned his mother had died at the age of 81. George wrote to his sister, Betty, that "awful, and affecting as the death of Parent is," their mother had enjoyed a long life in good mental and physical health.

Washington and his mother had not shared an easy relationship. Mary rarely expressed pride in her son's accomplishments and continually asked George for money. During the war she complained that she lived in poverty and requested the Virginia legislature pay her money as mother of the commander in chief. Humiliated, Washington stopped the action.

Washington had always provided his mother with a home, money, and goods. As Mary grew older, he encouraged her to move in with one of her children—just not with him. He wrote that Mount Vernon, with its ever-present visitors, "may be compared to a well resorted tavern." While Mary was welcome to come, he assured her she would not like all the strangers, and the company would prove too tiring for her.

A Visit with the President

Everyone clamored to see the president. People turned up at all hours and expected Washington to drop his pen and chat. Finally, unable to get through his work, Washington set limits. He didn't want to look snobbish, but enough was enough!

Every Tuesday afternoon from three to four o'clock, any man respectably dressed could drop in without an invitation and see Washington. Everyone stood on these occasions; the room too small for chairs to seat all the people. Washington usually wore a black suit and one of his dress swords. He talked to as many people as he could. But he hated to see everyone gawking at him.

George and Martha Washington with Nelly and Wash.

Library of Congress, LC-USZ62-24801

On Friday evenings gentlemen and ladies both attended Martha Washington's tea parties. Washington enjoyed these occasions more than the Tuesday afternoons. He always liked ladies' company. Martha remained seated while George worked the room. He made sure Abigail Adams, the vice president's wife, enjoyed a place of honor on Martha's right.

The Washingtons hosted official dinners every Thursday afternoon at four o'clock. They rotated guests, inviting government officials one time, friends the next, and foreign dignitaries the time after that. Sometimes Nelly Custis helped her grandparents entertain. Martha insisted Nelly practice playing her harpsichord each day. Nelly wrote to a friend she could not attend a party because members of the "Honorable Congress" were coming to dinner and "they like to hear musick."

One guest listed the dishes served at a presidential dinner: soup, fish, roasted and boiled meats, fowls, apple pies, puddings, iced creams, melons, peaches, and nuts. All this was washed down with wine as the president "drank to the health of every individual by name around the table." The ladies then retired to another room while the men stayed to talk. The guest described how Washington

Host a Tea Party

Martha's tea parties were one way the First Family entertained during the years Washington served as president. And the Washington family enjoyed tea every afternoon at about six o'clock.

People of Washington's time brewed tea using loose tea leaves; tea bags had not been invented yet. Washington's guests sipped their tea while munching pound cake, cookies, "sweetmeats" (dried fruits and nuts), and bread and butter.

Invite over some friends or family and host your own tea party.

Adult supervision required

Materials

Table to serve your tea and food; you can use a tablecloth and decorate with flowers, napkins, small plates, spoons, and butter knives

Teakettle or covered pan

Tea bags or a tea strainer and loose tea (try Earl Grey or Darjeeling tea)

Bread knife

Serving plates and bowls

Pound cake from the grocery store

Bread

Dried fruit: apricots, apples, peaches, etc.

Nuts: whole cashews, almonds, walnuts, or pecans

Butter

Strawberry jam (optional)

Teapot

Teacups or mugs

Sugar or sugar cubes

Set up your tea table. Fill the teakettle with cold water and bring the water to a boil on the stove. Hang 3 or 4 tea bags into the teapot, or add 1 spoon of loose tea leaves for each cup. Cut slices of pound cake and arrange them on a plate. Cut slices of bread into squares and put on another plate. Put out a bowl of dried fruit and nuts. Cut a stick of butter into neat squares and put on a plate. Let the butter soften at room temperature. You can also put out a bowl of strawberry jam to eat with the bread and butter.

Pour the boiling water into the teapot. Let the tea steep in the hot water for 3 or 4 minutes. If you used tea bags, pull them out. If you used loose leaves, hold a tea strainer over each cup to catch the tea leaves as you pour. Pour the brewed tea into the teacups and serve your guests. Offer sugar or sugar cubes to sweeten the tea.

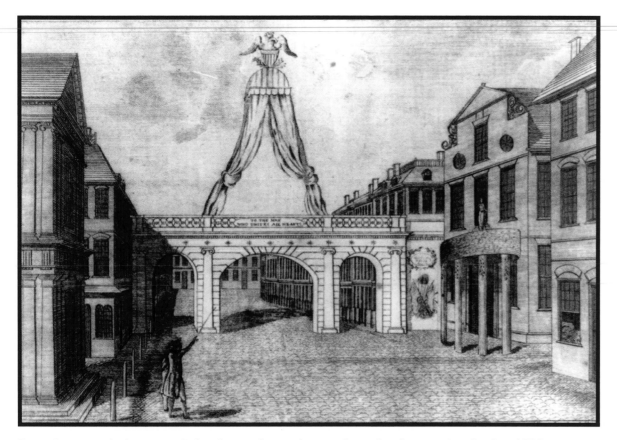

Boston's citizens built a triumphal arch to welcome the president when he visited in October 1789.

After five days, he began a slow climb back to health that left him too weak to work. He comforted himself in the knowledge that he had a group of capable advisors "who harmonize extremely well together."

Debts and Compromise

Washington sent a financial plan written by Secretary of the Treasury Alexander Hamilton to the second session of Congress. The plan focused on clearing up the states' Revolutionary War debts. Washington believed the federal government should pay these debts, because they had been made for the sake of all the states. Plus, he preferred having one federal plan instead of different plans in each state. But states like Virginia had already paid off their war debts. Why should they pay taxes to help states like Massachusetts that hadn't paid their debts?

The debate dragged on for months until Thomas Jefferson proposed a compromise that also resolved another burning issue: where the nation's permanent capital city should be built. Each region wanted the capital. Jefferson met with Hamilton and James Madison, an important leader in Congress. If Hamilton helped persuade the northern states to vote for a southern capital, Jefferson would swing southern votes to pass government "assumption" of the state debts.

kept a fork in his hand and tapped the edge of the table.

The Washingtons carefully chose what invitations they accepted. They enjoyed relaxing carriage rides around the city and attending the theater.

Washington toured through New England in autumn 1789. He scribbled notes on the region's booming trade, counted the numbers of ships, and visited little factories. People cheered Washington along the way but tiny things annoyed him. In Connecticut he couldn't travel on Sunday. And he disliked the way Massachusetts roads zigzagged around every farmer's field. Washington skipped visiting Rhode Island, which did not get around to approving the Constitution and joining the union until May 1790!

In 1790 doctors treated Washington for pneumonia and believed he lay near death.

Congress agreed to the compromise. Washington had the honor of choosing the site for the new capital, to be called the Federal City, somewhere along the Potomac River. In the meantime, the temporary capitol moved from New York City to Philadelphia.

Washington selected a site for the Federal City about 10 miles from Mount Vernon. In March 1791 Washington appointed a French engineer he'd known in the Continental Army, Pierre L'Enfant, to design and build the new capital. L'Enfant envisioned grand vistas, avenues radiating from central points, and monuments to American heroes. Streets would bear the names of states. The capitol and president's house would sit atop hills with a large street–Pennsylvania Avenue–connecting them. Washington loved the grandeur and beauty of L'Enfant's plan. Unfortunately, L'Enfant argued with too many people working on the project and Washington eventually had to replace him. In September 1793 Washington lay the corner-stone for the capitol building.

The Bank Bill

Hamilton next proposed creating a Bank of the United States to oversee the nation's debts and make loans for government projects. Local banks would follow policies set by the Bank of the United States. Hamilton hoped that bank policies would prevent the skyrocketing

The Washingtons' presidential homes in New York City and Philadelphia.

101

inflation seen during the war. The government, however, would only partly control the bank. The bank would also have investors. In this way, Hamilton's plan gave power and wealth to a group of private businessmen.

The bank bill passed the Senate. But in the House of Representatives James Madison argued that the Constitution did not give Congress the power to create a bank. The bill passed anyway and awaited Washington's signature.

Washington talked to Madison, and asked his cabinet for advice. Fellow Virginians Jefferson and Attorney General Edmond Randolph backed Madison. Hamilton, on the other hand, believed the Constitution "implied" that the government had the power to create a bank as part of its powers to regulate trade. He reasoned that if the Constitution didn't give government the chance to react to new situations, the document would soon be worthless.

Back when Madison championed the Constitution's adoption, he too had believed in "implied powers." He'd written in *The Federalist*, "Wherever a general power to do a thing is given, every particular power for doing it is included." Now, however, Madison (and his friend Thomas Jefferson) changed their views to a "strict interpretation"—only what was written in the Constitution could be carried out.

Washington listened carefully to Madison's words. But he agreed more with Hamilton's arguments. He signed the Bank Bill into law.

Harmony Turns Sour

Washington faced a troubling revolt in his own cabinet. The problems centered on Thomas Jefferson and Alexander Hamilton, brilliant men with strong personalities. Washington admired both men and had known them for years.

Thomas Jefferson served as Washington's first secretary of state.

Library of Congress, LC-USZ62-53985

A print based on a painting by Edward Savage shows Washington, Martha, Nelly, and Wash. Martha points with her fan to plans for the Federal City. The African American servant in the background could be Billy Lee, who rode with Washington throughout the war.

Courtesy of the Mount Vernon Ladies' Association

Political Parties, 1790s Style

At the time the United States was founded, a Federalist was someone who supported adopting the Constitution. The word came to mean those who supported the idea of a strong federal government. Federalists feared that too much power resting with the people could lead to mob rule and chaos. They did not trust the common man. A strong government, they felt, kept everyone happy under a rule of law, establishing order and peace. In foreign affairs, Federalists leaned toward Great Britain. They admired Britain's system of trade and centuries-old English law. Like Alexander Hamilton, Federalists supported an American economy that bolstered trade, small factories, and banking. The New England states became a stronghold for Federalist politicians.

Supporters of Thomas Jefferson became known as Jeffersonian Republicans or Democratic-Republicans, sometimes called simply Republicans. Unlike the Federalists, Republicans believed a strong central government threatened citizens' liberties. Power should rest with the people, which at the time meant white, property-holding, male voters. But as a nod to the fear of mob rule, Jeffersonian Republicans also felt that only a well-educated population could handle self-government. They also believed the country should stay a nation of farmers and not depend on New England Federalist strengths like trade and business. In foreign affairs, the Republicans favored France. They believed the French Revolution followed in the steps of liberty and freedom created by the American Revolution.

Over time, the political parties of the 1790s changed. The Federalist Party vanished, replaced in part by a party called the Whigs. The Whigs, too, would eventually disappear. Jefferson's Democratic-Republicans grew into the Democratic Party in the 1820s. The modern Republican Party was born in the 1850s as a northern political party opposed to the spread of slavery into the western territories.

Like Washington, Jefferson belonged to the southern aristocracy, a wealthy upper class whose members owned land worked by enslaved labor. Jefferson, who'd inherited land and slaves on his father's death, championed the agrarian life of the nation, a life based on land and farming. Like many southerners, Jefferson distrusted the northeastern states and their rival aristocracy of self-made merchants.

Hamilton was one of those self-made men. He'd been born with nothing, an illegitimate son abandoned by his father and orphaned by his mother's death. Hamilton promoted a far different future that included not only farming, but also factories, banks, stocks, and trade. Jefferson saw Hamilton as a vulgar upstart, even a dangerous man. Hamilton viewed Jefferson as a southern snob who preached equality he did not grant to others.

Jefferson's followers called themselves Democratic-Republicans or Republicans. Hamilton's supporters were called Federalists. Washington shared common beliefs with both men. He believed the United States needed an economy that mixed farming, trade, and manufacturing. He believed America's finances desperately needed strengthening. But Washington felt America, so rich in land, would stay a farming society for generations. And while he encouraged American factories, Washington felt Hamilton's radical 1792 *Report on Manufactures* went too far against "the temper of the times."

Unlike Jefferson, Washington never thought Hamilton's financial plans paved a road to monarchy in America. Washington believed a strong government and solid economy protected citizens' rights. Washington felt comfortable with Philadelphia's self-made merchants. He found them to be intelligent and hardworking people. He couldn't understand the level of distrust and dislike breeding between Hamilton and Jefferson.

Madison and Jefferson recruited Philip Freneau, a "poison-pen" journalist, to write articles attacking Hamilton in a Republican-backed newspaper called the *National Gazette*. Jefferson also paid Freneau to work in the state department. Freneau chipped away at Hamilton. He claimed that the secretary of the treasury meant to bury the nation in debt and create a monarchy, that Hamilton planned a "revolution in favor of the few. Another revolution must and will be brought about in favor of the people."

Meanwhile, Hamilton supported another newspaper, the *Gazette of the United States*, and published his own articles written under a different name. He claimed Jefferson spent government money to attack the government. He called for Jefferson's resignation and declared that Jefferson hoped to destroy the financial credit of the nation. Hamilton warned that Jefferson would let the country tumble into anarchy.

How Washington hated the war of words! He hated the charges flung back and

The masthead from Freneau's *National Gazette*.
Library of Congress, LC-USZ62-55677

forth "that stand in need of evidence for their support."

Washington finally asked Hamilton and Jefferson for their "explanations" and "complaints." Jefferson poured out his mistrust for Hamilton and his policies. He called Hamilton corrupt. Jefferson believed Hamilton's friends in Congress pocketed money for themselves and raised taxes at the same time. He wanted Hamilton's bank abolished; he believed it pressed southerners into debt to northern moneymen.

For his side, Hamilton claimed his plans created only good finances, not monarchy. He warned Washington that a political party swirled around Jefferson in the Congress. This party wanted to destroy Hamilton and through him, the government.

The split between Jefferson and Hamilton saddened Washington greatly. "I will frankly and solemnly declare that I believe the views of both of you are pure and well meant," he wrote to Jefferson in October 1792. Could the two men not make allowances for each other's opinions? "I . . . ardently wish that some line could be marked out by which both of you could walk." He wrote similar words to Hamilton. Without some yielding on both sides, Washington wrote, "I do not see how the Reins of Government are to be managed, or how the Union of the States can be much longer preserved. . . . Melancholy thought!"

Jefferson declared himself an innocent victim of Hamilton. The secretary of the treasury needed to change, not him. Jefferson lied when he told Washington he had not hired Freneau to attack the government. Jefferson now wondered if Washington, too, desired an American monarchy.

Hamilton admitted he wrote for the *Gazette of the United States*, but claimed it was only to protect his reputation. Out of affection for Washington, he promised "to smooth the path of your administration and to render it prosperous and happy."

Washington hated the bitter division between Hamilton and Jefferson.

Clashes in the West

Washington turned much of his attention to America's expanding frontier. For decades a stream of white settlers had steadily pushed Native American nations westward. After the war Americans swarmed west in even greater numbers. Clashes between Indians and settlers kept the frontier in flames. Great Britain encouraged this warfare to hurt the United States.

In his youth Washington had fought alongside and against Native Americans. Like most white men of the time, he had viewed the American Indians as bloodthirsty savages. Now, he saw native peoples more as "an unenlightened Race of Men." He hoped to find a solution other than warfare.

But Washington felt little hope for a peaceful frontier so long as whites stole Native American land and "our frontier Settlers entertain the opinion that there is not the same crime (or indeed no crime at all) in killing an Indian as in killing a white man." He pleaded with Congress to give "energy to the laws" throughout the frontier to stop "outrages upon the Indians." Without that, nothing else would ever achieve peace. Under pressure from the continued violence, however, Washington sent armies to subdue the warring western tribes in the Northwest Territory.

In 1790 Little Turtle of the Miami nation ambushed and defeated Josiah Harmer's force. The next year Little Turtle defeated the troops of General Arthur St. Claire. The United States lost 900 men in St. Claire's debacle, the worst defeat of a United States army at the hands of Native Americans. In 1794 General Anthony

General Anthony Wayne.

Wayne's well-planned and well-supplied force defeated Indian nations led by the Shawnee Blue Jacket at the Battle of Fallen Timbers near present day Toledo, Ohio. The next year Wayne imposed the Treaty of Greenville on the tribes. Native Americans gave up lands in Ohio, Illinois, Indiana, and Michigan.

Rumbles in Europe

Washington closely followed events in Europe, especially those in France. He felt proud that Lafayette was one of the leaders seeking new freedoms for the French people. "The renovation of the French Constitution is indeed one of the most wonderful events in the history of mankind," he wrote to historian Catherine Graham in January 1790.

Yet Washington knew that in unstable times, with mobs surging through Parisian streets, the situation could suddenly flash out of control. He hoped the "disorders [and] oppressions" would end "very much in favor of the rights of man." But in August 1791 King Louis XVI and Queen Marie Antoinette ended the reform movement. Captured while trying to flee Paris, the monarchs were forced to accept a new French constitution.

Revolutionary French forces threw the king and queen into prison. Violence engulfed Paris. A revolutionary government sat in charge. In 1792 France declared war on Austria, the homeland of Queen Marie Antoinette.

The situation in France drove another wedge through American politics. Most Americans supported France's march to liberty and freedom. Jefferson and the Republicans wholeheartedly championed France. The Federalists, a more conservative group, held back support, as chaos seemed the only master in France. But to Republicans this attitude proved Federalists favored monarchy over freedom.

Washington remained cautious. The Republican newspapers targeted his reluctance as the "offspring of inequality, begotten by aristocracy and monarchy." But Washington simply did not want his country sucked into dangerous European affairs.

Run, or Step Aside?

Under this cloud of division Washington debated whether he should stay for a second term as president. He'd survived several brushes with death, and at age 60 he'd outlived many in his family. He felt the strain; he felt old. He worried about his mind and his poor memory.

He told his cabinet he did not wish to run again. Let the experiment go forward. Show the world the United States could peacefully move power from one man to the next. Washington even wrote a list of points for a farewell address to the nation. "We are *all* the Children of the same country . . . Our interest, however diversified in local & smaller matters, is the same in all the great & essential concerns of the Nation." He emphasized that the economies of different regions made the nation stronger as a whole.

But from every corner advisors and friends insisted Washington must stay on. The country needed him. Washington, and Washington alone, could hold the country together. A female friend, Eliza Powell, wrote to Washington that people would believe "you would take no further risks" for the nation. Jefferson told

Washington, "North and South will hang together if they have you to hang on."

In the end, Washington felt he had no choice. He made no announcement to withdraw his name, and the Electoral College elected Washington unanimously to a second term.

Washington felt pressure to remain as president for a second term.

Library of Congress, LC-USZ62-96385

107

6

First in Their Hearts

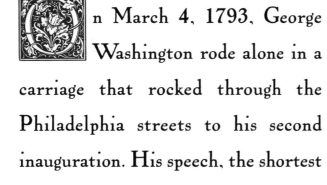n March 4, 1793, George Washington rode alone in a carriage that rocked through the Philadelphia streets to his second inauguration. His speech, the shortest inaugural address in history at 135 words, may also have been the gloomiest. He spoke of "Constitutional punishment" and "the upbraidings of all who now witness the present solemn ceremony" if he broke his oath of office. Gloomy indeed!

A few weeks later news poured in from Europe. The French government had beheaded King Louis XVI and declared a new French republic. While the monarchs of Europe reacted with horror, Washington formally

France's former king, Louis XVI, in a 1793 print, faces his death in Paris.

Library of Congress, LC-USZ62-99731

recognized the new French government. "We surely cannot deny to any nation," he wrote, "the right whereon our own government is founded, that every nation may govern itself according to whatever form it pleases."

More dark news soon arrived: Great Britain and France were at war, a war that spread across Europe, engulfing Austria, Prussia, Spain, and the Netherlands. Washington determined that the United States, which traded with both France and Great Britain, must remain neutral. His nation needed time to "improve without interruption the great advantages which nature" had "placed within our reach."

Washington's views meant little to the two superpowers. Great Britain, the world's mightiest sea power, seized American trade ships sailing to French ports. Great Britain also refused to turn over their frontier forts to the United States as promised in the treaty ending the American Revolution. From places like Fort Detroit the British supplied Native Americans with guns to fight the new nation's settlers.

France felt the United States owed them for their help during the American Revolution. If Washington put neutrality ahead of that debt, the French government aimed to whip up support and aid directly from the American people. Meanwhile, they planned to license privately owned ships to capture British trade vessels. These ships, called privateers, raided enemy ships, then divided the captured valuables with the French government. France wanted to use American harbors to equip privateer ships and hire American sailors eager for a share of captured wealth.

Washington rushed to protect American interests. On April 22, 1793, only 10 days after hearing France and Great Britain were at war, he issued an official Proclamation of Neutrality adopting "a conduct friendly and impartial towards the belligerent powers." If

Cut a Silhouette

A silhouette was a popular art form in the late 1700s.

Materials

Large sheet of white paper

Tape

Lamp or other bright light

Pencil

Scissors

Large sheet of black paper

Large sheet of colored paper, or
   another sheet of white paper

Glue

Sit in profile against a wall, and tape a large sheet of white paper to it at head level. Shine a bright light at the wall. (If you use a lamp you may have to take the lampshade off.) This will cast your shadow on the white paper. Move the light closer or farther away to make the shadow crisp and clear. Have someone trace your profile onto the white paper.

A silhouette of George Washington from around 1788.

Library of Congress, LC-USZ62-45514

*trace the shadow
and cut out*

*glue on black silhouette
white or colored paper*

Cut out your profile. Tape this white paper pattern onto the black sheet of paper and use it to cut out a black silhouette of your profile. Glue the black profile onto the final sheet of paper. Display your silhouette!

Washington receives the new French minister, "Citizen" Edmund Genet.

America meant to stay neutral, France could not outfit privateers or sell captured ships in the United States.

The pro-French Republican press ripped Washington's position. His neutrality, they charged, helped Britain and hurt France. The criticism distressed Washington, who felt he'd acted for the good of the country. Jefferson, who'd agreed to the Proclamation of Neutrality as a cabinet member, wrote to Madison that the attacks "extremely affected" Washington. But Washington was, claimed Jefferson, "enveloped in the rags of royalty," and those clothes couldn't be torn off without some scratches. The papers attacked Washington, wrote Jefferson, because of "the love of the people to France and its cause, which is universal."

Washington believed the United States must stand clear of Europe's web of war. And unlike the Republicans, he felt uneasy about the situation in France, where he believed government leaders "are ready to tear each other to pieces." Events proved Washington right. During 1793 and 1794, France's revolutionary government executed thousands of French citizens beneath the blade of the guillotine.

The new French government sent Edmund Genet as their minister to the United States. Encouraged by crowds of welcoming Americans, Genet soon stuck like a thorn in Washington's side. One of Genet's schemes called for an attack on Great Britain's ally,

Spain, in the Louisiana Territory. The idea of European powers fighting in the United States' backyard chilled Washington.

In July 1793 Washington learned Genet had secretly armed a privateer ship, recruited American sailors, and turned the vessel loose to attack British ships. Meanwhile, Genet organized groups called "democratic societies" to whip up support for France. Washington fumed. Had the troublesome Frenchman undercut American neutrality and dealt Great Britain an excuse to declare war on the United States?

The president and his entire cabinet, including Jefferson, decided France must recall Genet. Washington agreed to Jefferson's request to hide Genet's activities so France would not be embarrassed. But the never-ending attacks on Washington in the Republican papers had hit their mark. Jefferson recorded that the president "got into one of those passions when he cannot command himself." Washington, wrote Jefferson,

defied any man on earth to produce one single act of his since he had been in the government which was not done on the purest motives . . . by God he had rather be in his grave than in his present situation. That he had rather be on his farm than be made emperor of the world, and yet that they were charging him with wanting to be a king.

Jefferson warned the Republicans to back off. He feared a backlash against France and a surge in support for Washington's policy. At the same time, Hamilton and other Federalists could not keep quiet. They published letters declaring that the French minister meant to drag the United States into war. In the end, the French government recalled Genet. The new minister planned to send Genet back to France for a probable date with the guillotine. Washington graciously granted Genet asylum, allowing him to remain in the United States.

As 1793 drew to a close, Jefferson left his post as secretary of state. Washington knew that Jefferson had been a strong voice in the cabinet to balance Hamilton's equal strength. "The opinion that I formed of your integrity and talents," Washington wrote to Jefferson, "have been confirmed by the fullest experience." But Jefferson had often said one thing to Washington, then written against it to his Republican friends in Virginia. Jefferson could now devote himself to opposing the Federalists.

As the crisis with France eased, troubles flared over Great Britain's passage of the Provision Order, allowing British ships to capture vessels sailing to the French West Indies. Within a few months they'd captured over 250 American ships and confiscated the cargoes. The news infuriated Americans.

Washington sent John Jay, a Federalist, to attempt a "fair and firm negotiation" with Great Britain. He also sent James Monroe, a Republican, as his new minister to France. Washington expected both men to lay aside their own political feelings and serve as loyal representatives of his government. But Jay relied on advice from fellow Federalists on what treaty terms to seek. And Monroe wrote coded letters to Jefferson.

The Whiskey Rebellion

Not only foreign affairs claimed Washington's attention. In the summer of 1794, frontiersmen in western Pennsylvania revolted against a tax on whiskey. For many frontier families it proved easier to distill their grain into whiskey and tote the jugs to market instead of lugging bushels of grain. Whiskey was even traded in place of money.

The whiskey tax had been around since 1791, but now violence erupted; Washington believed Genet's democratic societies fueled the unrest. Class warfare spread as armed bands attacked the homes of wealthier citizens and whiskey tax collectors. They smashed the stills of anyone who paid the tax and branded some government officials with hot irons.

Washington could not allow armed bandits to terrorize law-abiding citizens or "there is an end put at one stroke to republican government, and nothing but anarchy and confusion is to be expected." And he feared the rebellion might spread. Still, Washington did not act hastily. Were there real complaints the government could

Washington greets people as he leaves church in 1795.

Library of Congress, LC-USZ62-32985

militias went home. But Washington further angered Republicans by declaring that the democratic societies meant to "shake the government to its foundation."

The Jay Treaty

In March 1795 John Jay's treaty with Great Britain reached the president. Britain promised to turn over the western forts by June 1796. The treaty settled old debts left over from the American Revolution. But Britain would continue to seize anything useful to France off American ships. The United States agreed to not let its ports be used by enemies of Great Britain. An important point Washington wanted were American rights to trade in the British West Indies. Britain agreed, but only for smaller American ships.

Washington knew the Republicans would howl that the treaty favored Great Britain, shattered neutrality, and hurt the United States. Without making any recommendations as to whether they should approve or reject it, Washington handed the Jay Treaty over to a special session of Congress on June 8. After an 18-day debate the Senate voted to ratify the treaty except for the clause about the West Indies trade. They wanted that point renegotiated. Now Washington had to decide whether to sign the treaty into law or not.

address? He sent commissioners to western Pennsylvania, and issued a proclamation asking people to return to their homes by September 1. Just in case, he called out the militia.

Republicans accused Washington of trampling the rights of simple farmers. Other Americans worried the Whiskey Rebellion offered but a taste of future violence, the kind of bloody chaos spread by the French Revolution. When the rebellion did not end, Washington himself led the militia into western Pennsylvania. Washington warned the soldiers to be "regardful of the rights of their fellow citizens." Courts, not the military, would try the criminals. The rebellion quickly faded. The

He packed his bags and headed for Mount Vernon. Letters arrived daily storming against the Jay Treaty. Washington's own opinion of the treaty was not favorable, but he believed it would keep the nation out of war. He also knew that accepting the treaty would encourage France to further interfere in United States business. He wrote to Hamilton, who'd also left the cabinet and returned to his law career in New York in early 1795. Washington asked Hamilton his opinion for and against each point of the treaty. In August Washington decided he would approve the Jay Treaty, but ask Great Britain for some changes.

New vacancies left Washington with cabinet posts to fill. Henry Knox and Alexander Hamilton were gone, as was Edmund Randolph, who had replaced Jefferson. But no one wanted the jobs! No one wished to become targets of the poisonous press. Washington finally filled the positions, with his third or fourth choices, and Vice President John Adams wrote, "The offices are once more filled but how differently when Jefferson, Hamilton, etc., were here!"

Showdown with the House of Representatives

On December 8, 1795, Washington traveled to the Senate chamber to give his yearly State of

Washington's Teeth

By 1789 George Washington had only one tooth of his own left in his mouth. He used sets of dentures, uncomfortable contraptions made of lead and set with human teeth and teeth carved from cow teeth and elephant ivory (not wood). The dentures were hinged with springs at the back of the mouth to open and close. Like the dentures worn by other people of his time, the false teeth distorted the shape of Washington's mouth.

In 1797 John Greenwood of Philadelphia repaired a set of Washington's dentures. The president worried about how he looked. "Nothing must be done to them which will, in the *least* degree force the lips out more than *now* do, as it does this too much already; but if both upper and lower teeth were to incline inwards more, it would shew the shape of the mouth better," he wrote to Greenwood.

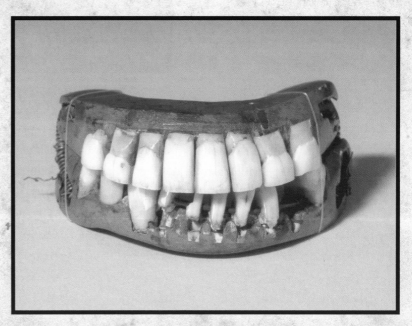

One of three surviving sets of Washington's dentures.

Courtesy of the Mount Vernon Ladies' Association

the Union address. Congressmen and senators waited tensely. How would the president defend the hated Jay Treaty? Instead, Washington stressed the good. Great Britain promised to leave the western forts. General Anthony Wayne had been victorious over the Indian tribes of the northwest. A nearly finished treaty with Spain would grant the United States use of the Mississippi River. And while European nations remained locked in war and dragged down by revolts at home, Washington reminded everyone, the United States enjoyed peace. "Is it too much to say that our country exhibits a spectacle of national happiness never before surpassed if ever equaled?"

On the Jay Treaty, Washington said he had used "the best judgment I was able to form of the public interest" and he had followed the Senate's advice. America's prosperity and peace did not depend on France or Great Britain, but in keeping the nation free to grow its own way.

To show their displeasure, House Republicans voted in February 1796 *not* to send Washington good wishes for his 65th birthday. They demanded Washington turn over all papers dealing with the Jay Treaty and its negotiations. The House of Representatives claimed they had the right to reconsider any treaty.

Washington debated what to do, and in the end refused. He had signed the treaty; it was the law of the land. Everything had been done according to the Constitution. Under the

Print of Washington based on a painting by Rembrandt Peale.

Constitution, the president, with the advice and consent of the Senate, negotiated treaties. Diplomacy, he wrote to the House members, required caution and even secrecy for success. Washington used care not to meddle with the other branches of government and he was not going to let the House meddle with the power of the president or the Senate.

In July 1796 Washington and Jefferson exchanged their last letter. Mixed in with bits about farming, Washington told Jefferson he

never believed he'd be accused of being an enemy of France and a puppet of Great Britain. He'd only wished "to preserve this Country from the horrors of a desolating war." Instead, every act of his administration was "tortured" and misrepresented "in such exaggerated and indecent terms as could hardly be applied to a . . . common pick pocket."

As Great Britain eased off the Provision Order and turned over the northwest posts, France reacted to the Jay Treaty. Encouraged by Washington's own minister, James Monroe, the French protested the treaty as an American alliance with Great Britain. French ships began harassing American trading vessels in the West Indies.

Again, a war of words broke out. One Republican writer wondered if Washington had "abandoned good principles or whether you ever had any." What could Washington do but protest that these writings "attach principles to me which every action of my life have given lie to!"

Leaving the Presidency

Sick of it all, Washington left for Mount Vernon. On his way out of town he dropped off a manuscript at *Claypoole's American Daily Advisor*. It was his farewell address to the nation. There were no laws limiting how many terms a president could have, but Washington knew no amount of arm-twisting could compel him to serve another one. The *American Daily Advisor* published Washington's paper on September 19, 1796. Other newspapers rushed Washington's words into print. The address spread from city to city and across the Atlantic.

Washington's Farewell Address, one of American history's great documents, touched on many subjects, including Washington's hopes and his warnings to the new nation.

On the Union: "The Unity of Government which constitutes you one People is also now dear to you. It is justly so; for it is a main Pillar in . . . your real independence, the support of your tranquility at home; your peace abroad; . . . of that very Liberty which you so highly prize."

On the Spirit of Political Parties:

This spirit, unfortunately, is inseparable from our nature having its root in the strongest passions of the human Mind. . . . It serves always to distract the Public Councils. . . . It agitates the Community with ill founded jealousies and false alarms, kindles the animosity of one part against another. . . . There is the opinion that parties in free countries are useful checks upon the Administration of the Government and serve to keep alive the spirit of Liberty. . . . But . . . in Governments purely elective, it is a spirit not to be encouraged.

On Foreign Influence: "Observe good faith and justice towds. all Nations. Cultivate peace and harmony with all. . . . 'Tis our true policy to steer clear of permanent Alliances, with any portion of the foreign world."

On Neutrality: "With me, a predominant motive has been to . . . gain time to our Country to settle and mature its yet recent institutions, and to progress without interruption, to that degree of strength and consistency, which is necessary to give it . . . the command of its own fortunes."

On Retirement: Washington promised himself "the sweet enjoyment of partaking, in the midst of my fellow Citizens, the . . . good Laws under a free Government, the ever favourite object of my heart, and the happy reward, as I trust, of our mutual cares, labours and dangers."

Washington made his final address to Congress on December 7, 1796. His term as president would end in three months. During the election Washington publicly favored no candidate, standing somewhere between Republican and Federalist. The United States must show the world the republican form of government worked, that power could move smoothly from one man to another without bloodshed, without a loss of liberty. In stepping down from the presidency after two terms Washington set a precedent followed by presidents for the next 130 years. John Adams, a Federalist, won the election. Republican Thomas Jefferson earned the second-most votes and became vice president.

John Adams.
Library of Congress, LC-USZ62-13002

During Adams's inauguration ceremony many eyes strayed to George Washington. A bit miffed, Adams wrote to his wife about "the full eyes, the streaming eyes, the trickling eyes" as people realized Washington would soon

Washington's 16-Sided Treading Barn

In 1792 work had begun on one of Washington's newest farm experiments—a 16-sided "treading barn" for thrashing wheat. Separating grain from straw was slow, hard work that required beating the stalk to break off the grain. Sometimes the wheat was laid on the ground, mixing with dirt, mud, and manure, while horses trampled over it and broke the grain from the straw.

Washington's treading barn protected the whole process from wet weather. Workers spread the wheat on the barn's second-story floor, a floor made of wooden slats spaced 1½ inches apart. Horses trotted around inside the barn, treading the grain out of the wheat. The grain fell through the slats into a brick room below, where it was swept up, bagged, and carted to Washington's gristmill for grinding into flour.

leave them. Adams noted Washington seemed peaceful and happy, as if enjoying "a triumph over me. Methought I heard him say 'Ay, I'm fairly out and you're fairly in. See which of us will be happiest!'"

Within days, the Washingtons left for Virginia. They shipped much of their baggage and belongings by boat to Mount Vernon. Fragile objects were squashed into the crowded carriage among George, Martha, Nelly, and Wash. "On one side, I am called upon to remember the parrot [Nelly's pet]; on the other, to remember the dog. For my own part, I should not pine if they were both forgot," wrote Washington. The family arrived home on March 15, 1797.

Home Again

"I find myself in the situation, nearly, of a young beginner," Washington wrote to a friend a few weeks later. Everything was a mess! House, barns, and fields all needed attention. Instead of increasing in size, his herds of horses and cattle and flocks of sheep had shrunk during his eight-year absence. Much of his land, cracked and eroded, needed loving attention, too.

Washington hired bricklayers, carpenters, and painters, then grumbled when they were

Nineteenth-century illustration of Mount Vernon.
Library of Congress, LC-USZ62-93527

not at work as early as he. The "Music of hammers" and paint fumes haunted nearly every room. Daily, Washington rode his farms until mid-afternoon dinner. At the table, "I rarely miss seeing strange faces; come, as they say, out of respect to me. Pray, would not the word curiosity answer as well?"

Instead, Washington wished for just a few good friends he could laugh and talk with. But many of his close friends had died or moved away. The younger Virginian politicians flocked to Jefferson. Washington wrote to Sally Fairfax, now a widow living in London, encouraging her to return to Virginia. All the great events of his life, he wrote, could not fade his memories "of those happy moments, the happiest in my life, which I have enjoyed in your company."

Washington began selling his western lands to raise cash to restore his farms. His lands in the Shenandoah Valley and western Pennsylvania, some owned since he was a teenager, were worth many times what he'd paid. But few buyers seemed interested, forcing Washington to sell some lands below their value. In explaining this situation to one of his nephews seeking a loan, Washington complained, "You are under the same mistake that many others are, in supposing that I have money always at Command." Still, he loaned the money to his nephew.

Politics Won't Let Go

Washington continued following the political situations at home and in Europe. He had tried so hard to remain neutral and above the developing spirit of political parties. Now, he sided firmly with the Federalists. He was furious when the French government refused to accept commissioners sent by President Adams unless the commissioners paid France a bribe. Washington believed the Republicans would only be happy when the United States bowed to France's control.

In fact, during 1798 fear grew that France might invade the United States. President Adams, a loud critic of France, called on Washington to resume his role of commander in chief if needed. In November 1798 Washington traveled to Philadelphia to create plans for an army. The crisis passed, however, without the nation needing Washington's military skills.

As he grew older, the political ideals that had guided Washington for so many years seemed to fade. He feared the "best qualified" men "will not come forward" to run for office. He wondered if the only qualification to become president was to be the candidate of the more powerful political group. A party might "set up a broomstick and call it a true son of liberty, a democrat, or give it any other epithet that will suit their purpose, and it will command their votes." What would happen when one party "hangs upon the wheels of Government as a dead weight, opposing every measure"?

Washington's Will

In July 1799 George Washington wrote his final will. Without children of his own, he divided his estate among his nieces and nephews and Martha's grandchildren. He left

Washington's 16-sided barn was still standing when this photograph was taken in 1870. Today, a working reproduction can be visited at Mount Vernon.

Courtesy of the Mount Vernon Ladies' Association

119

Make Nelly's Hoecakes

George Washington enjoyed hoecakes and tea for breakfast nearly every morning. Here is a version of Nelly Custis's recipe for hoecakes. It makes two dozen 3-inch hoecakes.

Adult supervision required

Ingredients and Utensils

Round 24-ounce container of white
    cornmeal
Measuring cup
1 teaspoon dry yeast
Mixing bowl
Warm water
Plastic wrap
1 egg
Pinch of salt
Griddle or skillet
Spatula
Shortening
Butter
Honey or syrup

Mix 2 cups of cornmeal with the dry yeast in a mixing bowl. Add enough warm water to make a pancake-like batter. Cover the bowl with plastic wrap and let it rest on the counter overnight.

In the morning, slowly stir in the rest of the cornmeal. Add the egg and more warm water to make it the consistency of pancake batter. Add a pinch of salt. Let the mixture sit for 20 minutes.

Heat a griddle or skillet until a few drops of water dance on the surface. Grease the griddle with a spoonful of shortening. Spoon the batter onto the hot griddle and lightly press it flat with the spatula. Be sure to stir the batter again before spooning out each cake. Flip the hoecake when it turns golden brown on the bottom side.

Serve warm with butter and honey— just like George Washington ate them.

his jewel, Mount Vernon and 4,000 acres, to his nephew Bushrod, a future U.S. Supreme Court justice. Washington forgave all the debts owed to him. He donated money to establish a university. To friends and family he left gifts: his presidential desk and chair, his spyglass, his telescope, and a gold-headed cane given to him by Benjamin Franklin. He left Lafayette a set of pistols taken from the enemy during the Revolution.

One of the first sections of Washington's will stated that upon Martha's death, "It is my Will and desire that all the Slaves which I hold in my own right, shall receive their freedom." Former slaves too old or sick to support themselves in freedom would be fed and clothed by his estate "while they live." Children without parents who could care for them should be taught a trade or useful skill as well as reading and writing. Washington directed his heirs to see that this was done "without evasion, neglect, or delay."

By freeing his slaves Washington hoped to set an example that other Americans, especially his fellow Virginians, might follow. But other leaders and future presidents like Jefferson, Madison, and Monroe, who talked eloquently about liberty and the rights of man, did not free their slaves.

Washington's views on slavery had changed during and after the American Revolution. At first he was shocked by New England's use of free blacks in the militia, but as the war dragged on Washington used both free blacks and eventually enslaved blacks. Some slaves exchanged service in the army for freedom after the war.

Time in the North also exposed Washington to economies that did not rely on enslaved labor as in the South. (After the Revolution northern states gradually ended slavery, freeing a slave when he or she reached a certain age.) As president Washington encouraged manufacturing and banking to help diversify the new nation's economy.

Washington wrote to a friend in September 1786, "I never mean . . . to possess another slave by purchase; it being among my first wishes to see some plan adopted, by the legislature by which slavery in this Country may be abolished by slow, sure . . . degrees." In a letter that same year to Lafayette, Washington praised the Frenchman's desire to free the slaves. "Would to God," wrote Washington, "a like Spirit could diffuse itself generally into the minds of the people of this country, but I despair of seeing it—some petitions were presented to the Assembly at its last Sessions, for the abolition of slavery, but they could scarcely obtain a reading."

So why didn't Washington free his own slaves earlier? Why did he wrestle with the issue for so long? Perhaps one reason was that Washington knew slavery had the power to tear the nation apart—as it would 60 years after his death, in the Civil War.

Washington on Love

George Washington often offered advice to his nephews and nieces and Martha's grandchildren. He covered all topics, from picking up their clothes, to schoolwork, to love. To step-granddaughter Elizabeth Parke Custis he noted, "Love is too dainty a food to live upon alone" and should be only one ingredient of a good marriage. He advised Nelly Custis:

[Love] ought to be under the guidance of reason. . . . When the fire is beginning to kindle, and your heart growing warm, propound these questions to it. Who is this intruder? Have I a competent knowledge of him? Is he a man of good character; a man of sense? For be assured, a sensible woman can never be happy with a fool.

A few years later, in 1799, Nelly married Washington's nephew Lawrence Lewis on her grandfather's birthday. Sadly for Nelly, her husband never measured up to the grandfather she adored.

Washington waits to escort Nelly Custis to her wedding while Martha follows her granddaughter down Mount Vernon's staircase.

Create a Commemorative Sword

To each of his nephews Washington gave one of his swords, reminding them "not to unsheathe them for the purpose of shedding blood, except it be for self-defense, or in defense of their County and its rights."

Adult supervision required

Materials

Rectangular Styrofoam board from a craft store, long enough to make a sword

Black marker

Sharp knife

Gold metallic paint

Brush

Aluminum foil

Tape

Draw your sword onto the Styrofoam board with the marker. With adult help, use the sharp knife to saw through the board, cutting out your sword. Paint the handle on the sword gold. Let it dry, and paint another coat. Let the second coat dry. Wrap the sword blade with aluminum foil and tape into place. Try not to get the foil too wrinkled. Use the marker to draw a line down the center of the foil-covered blade, as shown. Use the marker to add details to the sword's gold handle.

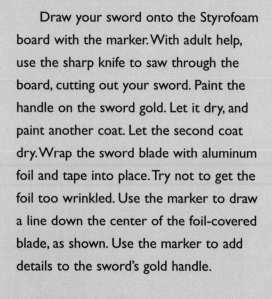

Styrofoam board

drawn sword

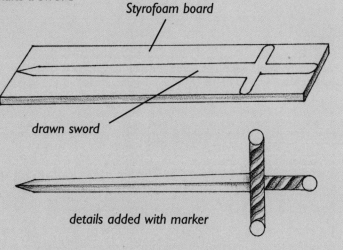

details added with marker

Washington also worried about how freed African Americans would survive having lived without education and without the responsibilities of freedom. He wrote to David Humphreys:

The unfortunate condition of the persons whose labors I inpart employed has been the only unavoidable subject of regret. . . . To lay a foundation to prepare the rising generation for a destiny different from that in which they were born, affords some satisfaction to my mind, & could not I hoped be displeasing to the justice of the Creator.

In December 1793 Washington wrote to Tobias Lear about a scheme "to liberate a certain species of property which I possess, very repugnantly to my own feelings." He planned to rent his lands to skilled English farmers. These farmers would pay Washington's freed slaves to work for them. But there was no interest in his plan.

Like other slave owners, Washington had a lot of money invested in slavery. Most slave owners easily raised cash by selling slaves. But Washington had decided in the 1770s he would no longer sell slaves and break up families without the slave's permission. Unlike many slave owners, Washington encouraged his slaves to marry—although the state of Virginia did not recognize slave marriages. Many of the slaves he owned were married to slaves he'd acquired through his marriage to Martha.

These slaves belonged to the Custis estate, and Washington could not free them. This posed a problem Washington wrestled with unsuccessfully for years.

In the end, unsure how to free his slaves, unsure how to prepare his slaves for freedom, he put off the decision until his death.

"I Die Hard"

December 12, 1799, dawned gray and cold, the sky spitting snow and icy rain. As usual Washington rose early, bundled into his coat, and rode around his five farms supervising the day's work. By the next day he'd developed a bad cold and a sore throat. Tobias Lear suggested he take medicine and go to bed, but Washington brushed the idea aside.

Washington woke sometime in the early morning hours of Saturday, December 14, straining to breathe. He waited until morning, then sent for his doctors, including James Craik, who'd been his friend since that time long ago at Fort Necessity.

Washington's three doctors attempted to rid his body of the illness, which they diagnosed as quinsy, through bleeding and purging. They bled him four different times, taking nearly five pints of blood from his veins. They dosed him with medicines to bring on vomiting. Lear recorded that trying to swallow medicine almost suffocated Washington. As the

Washington died at Mount Vernon on December 14, 1799.

day dragged on Washington did not improve. By modern standards, the treatments must have severely weakened his body, already fighting a vicious virus.

Through a swollen throat Washington apologized for the trouble he caused those around him. He lay or sat in pain, often fighting for breath. He knew he was dying. At one point he whispered, "I die hard but am not afraid to go." He directed Martha to fetch his updated will and made sure people knew what to do with his papers. Even at the end he worried how his fellow citizens would judge him.

Darkness fell over Mount Vernon. Hushed servants lit the candles and huddled in the doorway. Several times Washington tried to tell Lear not to let him be buried until he'd been dead for two days. He had a sudden fear of being buried alive. Lear told him he would honor his request. "'Tis well," murmured Washington. Sometime between 10 and 11 o'clock that night George Washington died.

From the foot of their bed Martha asked, "Is he gone?"

Tobias Lear stood near Washington's head. Choked with tears, he held up his hand.

Illustrious Washington!

News of Washington's unexpected and sudden death sent shock waves across the land. One man claimed it felt as if the whole nation had

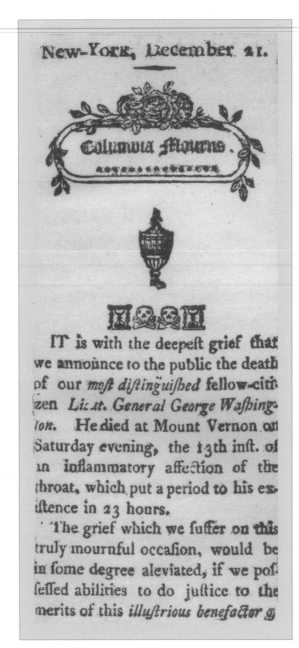

The New York Gazette and General Advertiser, *trimmed in mourning black, announces Washington's death.*

Etching from 1800 shows Columbia and Justice in mourning while Fame blows a trumpet announcing Washington's death.

lost their father at exactly the same moment. The *Virginia Gazette* published: "Still be the Voice of Mirth! Hushed be all Sounds of Joy! . . . Thy worthiest, noblest Son is no more–ILLUSTRIOUS WASHINGTON is dead!"

The nation sank into a period of official mourning that lasted until Washington's birthday: February 22, 1800. In hundreds of towns, large and small, mock funeral processions shuffled through the streets. Washington's friend Bryan Fairfax wrote, "Yes, he is gone, but he died, as he lived, with fortitude, so that he was great to the last."

From his first surveying job to his last days riding his farms, George Washington pushed himself to succeed. As a young man ambition burned within him. He thirsted for approval and recognition. All his life he held his honor and reputation dear. His need for approval left him sensitive to criticism; he especially felt stung when others questioned his motives. And when fame and leadership fell upon him, George Washington suffered moments of doubt, fearing he'd fail and lose the respect of those around him.

Washington led by example, relying on his determination, courage, and great physical strength. No detail was too small for his attention. He treated famous men and common folk with courtesy. His promise meant something. People trusted Washington's honor and fairness and turned to him again and again.

George Washington *was* the man to lead a successful Revolution. He *was* the man who could lead the effort to create a new Constitution. And finally, Washington was the single man his countrymen expected to lead them as their first president. Success or failure of an entire nation so often rested on Washington's shoulders.

One of Washington's doctors carefully measured his body so a coffin could be made:

6′ 3½″ length, 1′ 9′ across the shoulders, 2′ 9″ across the elbows with his arms folded. On December 18 mourners laid George Washington to rest at Mount Vernon. The day after Christmas Henry Lee remembered his friend before Congress, summing up Washington's impact with a few simple words:

"First in war, first in peace, and first in the hearts of his countrymen."

Resources

Glossary

amendment: a formal change to the Constitution requiring approval of three-fourths of the states to become law; the Bill of Rights is the first 10 amendments to the Constitution

assembly: the legislature of a state or colony; also, the term for a dance or ball

bayonet: a dagger-like weapon attached to the muzzle of a musket

colony: a separate territory belonging to or under the control of a nation, like Great Britain's 13 colonies in North America

democracy: a government in which the people hold power, either directly, or indirectly through representatives elected by the citizens

dysentery: a disease; severe diarrhea with blood and mucus

federal government: the central government of a nation, which has power to act on behalf of the states on issues that affect all the nation's citizens

Federalists: people who supported adopting the Constitution and a strong central government

House of Burgesses: the legislature of the colony of Virginia

legislature: an organized body of people empowered to make laws

militia: citizens who practice military maneuvers part time and are called to action during an emergency, then go home. A standing army is made up of trained, professional soldiers doing their full-time job.

mutiny: refusal to obey military orders; an uprising against the commanding officer

Parliament: the supreme legislative body of Great Britain, made up of the House of Commons and the House of Lords

republic: a type of democracy in which the people have power through their elected representatives

Republicans: supporters of a republic, or followers of Thomas Jefferson during Washington and Adams's terms as president

repeal: to do away with or take back a law by legislative action

Places to Visit and Web Resources

Places to Visit

Historic Mount Vernon, George Washington's Estate and Gardens
3200 Mount Vernon Memorial Highway
Mount Vernon, Virginia 22121
(703) 780-2000
www.mountvernon.org

Visit Washington's home, grave, gardens, and farm, plus a new interactive museum and exhibits. Web site has time lines, biographies, articles, virtual tour, and more.

Independence National Historical Park

143 South Third Street

Philadelphia, Pennsylvania 19106

(215) 965-2305

www.nps.gov/inde

Washington served here in the Continental Congress and the Constitutional Convention.

Point State Park

101 Commonwealth Place

Pittsburg, Pennsylvania 15222

(412) 471-0235

www.dcnr.state.pa.us/stateparks

Stand at the Forks of the Ohio River just as young Washington did. Today the area is a Pennsylvania state park with a museum; you can see where Fort Pitt and Fort Duquesne played a part in the French and Indian War.

Fort Necessity National Battlefield

One Washington Parkway

Farmington, Pennsylvania 15437

(724) 329-5512

www.nps.gov/fone

Visit a replica of the fort in the Great Meadow; see Jumonville Glen and Braddock's grave and a new visitor's center and museum.

Yorktown Battlefield
Colonial National Historical Park

Yorktown, Virginia 23690

(757) 898-2410

www.nps.gov/colo/

See where Cornwallis surrendered to Washington.

Colonial Williamsburg

The Colonial Williamsburg Foundation

P.O. Box 1776

Williamsburg, Virginia 23187-1776

(757) 229-1000

www.history.org

Step back in time to visit the Governor's Palace, the House of Burgesses, and the shops and taverns that Washington visited.

George Washington Birthplace National Monument

1732 Popes Creek Road

Colonial Beach, Virginia 22443

(804) 224-1732

www.nps.gov/gewa

See the outline of the foundation of the original Washington house. A house built in the 1930s as a "replica" of George's birthplace is much larger and grander than the real Washington home. Visit the Washington family burial ground. An untouched quiet, lovely park.

Valley Forge National Historical Park

1400 North Outerline Drive

King of Prussia, Pennsylvania 19406

(610) 783-1077

www.nps.gov/vafo

See Washington's headquarters and soldiers' huts and visit the museum at a place that came to symbolize the suffering of the Continental Army.

Morristown National Historical Park

30 Washington Place

Morristown, New Jersey 07960

(908) 766-8215

www.nps.gov/morr

The Continental Army spent two horrible winters at Morristown as they kept an eye on the British in New York.

Web Resources

Other National Park Service Revolutionary War sites: www.nps.gov/revwar

George Washington Papers at the Library of Congress: www.loc.gov

The Papers of George Washington at the University of Virginia: www.virginia.edu/gwpapers

The original Declaration of Independence, Bill of Rights, and Constitution at the National Archives: www.archives.gov

Resource Books for Kids

Allen, Thomas B. *George Washington, Spy Master*. Washington, DC: National Geographic Society, 2004.

Harness, Cheryl. *George Washington*. Washington, DC: National Geographic Society, 2000.

Herbert, Janis. *The American Revolution for Kids*. Chicago: Chicago Review Press, 2002.

Holt, Larry. *George Washington: A Photographic Story of a Life*. New York: DK Biography, 2005.

Meltzer, Milton. *George Washington and the Birth of Our Nation*. New York: Franklin Watts, 1986.

Miller, Brandon Marie. *Declaring Independence: Life During the American Revolution*. Minneapolis: Lerner Publishing, 2005.

Miller, Brandon Marie. *Growing Up in Revolution and the New Nation, 1775–1800*. Minneapolis: Lerner Publishing, 2002.

Yoder, Carolyn P., ed. *George Washington, the Writer: A Treasury of Letters, Diaries, and Public Documents*. Honesdale, PA: Boyds Mills Press, 2003.

Selected Additional Resources

Abbot, William, Dorothy Twohig, et al, eds. *The Papers of George Washington*. Charlottesville, VA: University of Virginia Press, 1976 and continuing.

Dalzell, Robert F, and Lee Baldwin. *George Washington's Mount Vernon: At Home in Revolutionary America*. New York: University of Oxford Press, 1998.

Fitzpatrick, John, ed. *The Last Will and Testament of George Washington*. Mount Vernon, VA: Mount Vernon Ladies' Association, 1932.

Flexner, James Thomas. *Washington the Indispensable Man*. New York: Little, Brown, 1969.

Kent, Donald H., ed. "George Washington's Journal for 1754," *Pennsylvania History* 19, no. 1 (January 1952).

Pogue, Dennis. "George Washington: Slave Master." *American History*, February 2004.

Rees, James. *Mount Vernon Commemorative Guidebook 1999, George Washington Bicentennial*. Mount Vernon, VA: Mount Vernon Ladies' Association, 1999.

Rhodehamel, John, ed. *The American Revolution: Writings from the War of Independence*. New York: Library of America, 2001.

Rhodehamel, John, ed. *Washington: Writings*. New York: Library of America, 1997.

Smith, Richard Norton. *Patriarch: George Washington and the New American Nation*. New York: Houghton Mifflin, 1993.

Thompson, Mary. "The Hospitable Mansion: Hospitality at George Washington's Mount Vernon." Mount Vernon Ladies' Association, paper presented 2003.

Washington, George. *The Journal of Major George Washington . . . To the Commandant of the French Forces on Ohio . . . October 1753–January 1754*. Williamsburg, VA: Colonial Williamsburg Foundation, 2004.

Washington, George. *George Washington's Rules of Civility and Decent Behavior in Company and Conversation*. Bedford, MA: Applewood Books, 1988. (This book reprints Washington's 110 Rules, which 14-year-old George copied from an English translation of a French book of manners.)

Index

Page numbers in italics denote illustrations.